Jurisprudence & Legal Theory

Outlines, Diagrams, & Exam Study Sheets

VisuaLaw Study Guide Volume 10

Markus McDowell

SULIS
INTERNATIONAL

Los Angeles | London

This VisuaLaw Study Guide is based on the University of London Study Guide for Jurisprudence. It is an independent work and is not connected with nor endorsed by the University.

Published by Sulis International
www.SulisInternational.com

JURISPRUDENCE: OUTLINES, DIAGRAMS, & EXAM STUDY SHEETS

ISBN-13: 978-1537239910
ISBN-10: 1537239910

First Edition: August 2016

1. Law 2. Jurisprudence

Contents

PREFACE

Welcome to VisuaLaw Study Guide Volume 10: Jurisprudence and Legal Theory. This book is divided into three sections: Outlines, Diagrams, and Exam Study Sheets. Each section covers the same material with different approaches and purposes.

Research shows that mere repetition and memorization is not enough to understand a subject well enough to take a law exam. A student must internalize the material and be able to recall details based on connections. These study guides are based on these principles.

Outlines are detailed outlines of the course material, arranged by topic, including statutes, cases, and key terms, arranged for aid in studying, memorizing, and revising/reviewing. Use these along with your textbook and other readings as you learn.

Diagrams are companions to the Course Outlines. These contain flow charts, diagrams, and other visual aids for each topic. Use these as a way to get the 'big picture' of each topic, and to test yourself by seeing if you can remember the details from the Outlines. Try re-drawing the diagrams from memory. (These are available as a separate eBook for Kindle Fire entitled *Jurisprudence: Diagrams for Law Students*).

Exam Study Sheets are condensed outlines, based on the Course Outlines. These can be used as another way of getting the big picture, but also for revising and testing yourself on the details. Each "sheet" contains 1–5 pages on each of the topics, including key statutes and cases.

The VisuaLaw Study Guides are not a substitute for required readings or any other assignments. Everything you need to know to pass the exams is not included—this book is an outline of the subject and a companion study tool. If you understand and can discuss each element on each page, you will be well on your way to understanding the subject.

Send questions, errata, and suggestions to legal.yankee@Sulis-Inc.com. Your input will help us continue to update and refine these study guide.

For updates and more legal education resources and information, join the Legal Yankee Law Student Mailing List at: http://eepurl.com/bwNJUL

COURSE OUTLINES

These Outlines present the topics and subtopics of the course in standard outline form, along with key terms, cases, and statutes.

Suggested study plan:

1. Look over the chapter which corresponds to the section you are about to study for your course.
2. Read your assigned readings and do any assigned activities. Periodically review the material in this Study Guide to reinforce the material.
3. Review the VisuaLaw Course Outline. Test yourself: are you able to discuss each item in detail? Go back over your reading material to strengthen the areas in which you are weak. Repeat until you have mastered the topic.
4. Repeat for each subject in the course.

When you are preparing for your exams, use the VisuaLaw Course Outlines to review the material you need to know, and guide you back to your course textbook and readings for the information you need to review.

1. Introduction

1.1 Studying Jurisprudence

Jurisprudence is more akin to studying philosophy or theology than most other legal courses you will take. It concerns itself with the "why" of law more than the "how."

Since it is a subset of philosophy, your study will involve learning about scholars, theories, and the pros and cons of each. You will seek to understand more than memorize; to be able to critique more than list.

1.2 Methodology

Because this is philosophy, it requires you to become intimate with the issues and concepts in order to do well on a test. Immersion is the key. Often, you will not understand an explanation or theory when you first read it. Push on. Read the textbook, read the source material, and use this outline. (Buy the companion Diagrams book, or make your own.) Reread everything. See if you can explain it to others.

After a while, you will begin to notice that you are slowly growing in your understanding. By the end of the course, if you stay with it, you will be able to converse in detail—explain the theories, critique them in detail, and add your own commentary.

Good luck in your studies and preparation.

2. The Nature of Legal Theory

2.1 Definition of Jurisprudence

- It addresses issues of legal philosophy, political morality, sociology, and history.
- Some outstanding thinkers have applied themselves to this field, describing either how things are, or how they should be.
- Various theories have been put forth by these scholars, and subscribed to by those who study them.
- The theories contribute to our understanding of how law works and how it should work.
- The theories contribute to how judges and lawyers think and approach the law as a whole.

2.2 Methodology, Analysis, Theory, Definition

- Descriptive theories: things as they are
- Normative theories: how things ought to be, or how people ought to behave, or must, or should behave.
- A theory can be both Descriptive and Normative: it both describes how things are, *and* how they should be.
- A descriptive theory can address the normative: we can describe it and then discuss what should or should not be done.

2.3 Theory and Evaluation

- John Mitchell Finnis (born 28 July 1940) notes '…that the evaluation of theorist are an indispensable and decisive component in the selection or formation of any concepts for use in description of such aspects of human affairs such as law or legal order.' (*Natural Law and Natural Rights*, chapter 1)
- I.e., the concept of baldness can be an observation (a person with little or no hair), but it can be a value (a senior citizen, a Neo-Nazi).
- H.L.A. Hart (18 July 1907 – 19 December 1992) chooses a comprehensive conception of law over narrow one.

2.4 The 'Interpretive' Approach

- Concepts are a loosely defined and uncontroversial, like a dictionary definition. Describing.
- This is distinct from "conceptions," which are theoretical constructs.

2.5 Summary

- Jurisprudence contains a lot of deep questions of methodology.
- Important to be aware of the various approaches devised by scholars and movements.
- But then a student must move from what other people have said, to what *he* or *she* thinks about each theory, construct, approach.

3. Hobbes, Bentham, and Austin: Imperative Theory (Command Theory)

3.1 Thomas Hobbes and the Beginnings of Positivism

- Thomas Hobbes of Malmesbury (5 April 1588 – 4 December 1679)
- Founder of liberalism, a reaction against medieval view where God was Creator and any discussion of society or law had to take that into account.
- Hobbs moved the debate to a more secular foundation—government, law, and society are what humans do.
- He is sometimes called the father of legal positivism, though he lived a couple of hundred years before the theory was actually described in modern terms.
- His book, *Leviathan*, was published in 1651.
  - Legitimacy of government is founded on humanity's nature
  - The greatest enemy is social chaos;
  - The natural condition of humankind is 'solitary, poor, nasty, brutal, and short.'
  - As rational creatures, we accept that a strong government is needed
  - This is the 'social contract.'

- (See Hart's analysis of the "Human Condition" below)

3.2 Jeremy Bentham

- Jeremy Bentham (15 February 1748 – 6 June 1832)
- Government has the rcsponsibility to organize civil society and interaction; the law is the path to do this.
- Bentham was a reformer whose goal was 'the greatest happiness of the greatest number is the foundation of morals and legislation.'
- 'Enlightened self-interest' is the key to understanding ethical behavior and norms.
- His book, *Introduction to Principles of Morals and Legislation* was published in 1789
- He pushed the idea of a total institution which he called the *panopticon.*
    - This ideal institution would have complete and perfect control over society and the citizens
    - Would be visible and involved in every aspect of social life.

3.3 John Austin

- John Austin (3 March 1790 – 1 December 1859)
- To achieve legal reform, one must understand the nature of law itself. This is what Austin attempted to do.
- Austin is remembered for his version of legal positivism, the 'command theory of law.'
- His theory drew upon Hobbs and Bentham.
- An ardent proponent of utilitarianism.

Lasting Contributions

- Analytical jurisprudence. Studies of law in terms of history or sociology should be secondary to analytical analysis.
  - Emphasized understanding of key concepts of law, right, duty, and legal validity.
  - This was a first step, a separate task, from understanding the concepts of law and the morality of law.
- Legal positivism. Law and jurisprudence should be an object of scientific study, not as a branch of moral or political theory, as those before him had argued.

Command theory

- Law is the creation of a sovereign (government)
- The goal is to achieve a rational, coherent, and defendable rule.
- Commands: an order that something be done, and a sanction (he called it 'evil') to be imposed if it is not done.
- Rules: general commands applied to a class, rather than specific or individual commands.
- Sovereign: a person or collection of persons who received habitual obedience from the majority of people, but does not habitually obey any other person or organization.
- Positive Law is contrasted with 'laws by close analogy' (positive morality, laws of honor, international law, customary law, constitutional law) and 'laws by remote analogy' (laws of physics, etc.)

Criticisms

- See Hans Kelsen's pure theory of law (Chapter 10), which is also an interpretive theory (and makes for widening the scope for an exam answer on the subject).
- It can be difficult to identify a "sovereign" in some cases.
- New rulers do not come into power with the habitual obedience from the citizens/subjects.
- The command model does not fit some aspects of law very well (laws that grand powers, will and trusts, contract law, etc.)
- Because it portrays law solely concerning power, it cannot distinguish between rules of terror and just rules—the only criteria is that they are accepted as legitimate by their own citizens.

4. Natural Law Theory

4.1 Ancient Greece and Rome

- Natural law tradition came from the application of the theory of morality, which emphasized humanity's universal moral nature to the legitimacy of the state.
  - When states sought to rule over different people with different customs, authority and legitimacy of the state are important.
  - Actual law seemed the way to provide a universal standard of justice for diverse people.
- Different natural law theories came about, however, which do not agree on what the universal basis of morality is.
  - Some focused on the intellect of human beings
  - or their reason
  - others on the purpose,
  - on the revelation of God's will.
- "Natural Law" is a misleading term. Initially, it explained the nature of morality.
  - Humans, using reason (perhaps with the help of the gods), could come to understand how to act properly.
  - It took account of man's nature (thus *natural* law).

- Today the term more often refers to the part which explains how the law, narrowly construed, operates as part of a larger moral life.
  - (The most important contemporary natural lawyer, John Finnis, says that the philosophy of law is continuous with general moral or ethic philosophy.)
- In small, primitive societies, there is no distinction between morality and what they think is the right way to do things—they have no external view of their practices.
  - Conflicts of customs occur when differing cultures interact.
  - The philosophies of Socrates, Plato, Aristotle, and the Stoics was carried via Rome throughout the world, and raised questions of "how ought a human to live?" and then philosophers sought a common nature and answer.
- A form of this is reflected in phrase *lex injusta non est lex* ("an unjust law is not law").
  - Positivists disagree—they say it is still law
  - (but they do not deny morality plays a role in law)
  - Bentham is an example: he was an arch-positivist and a reformer.

4.2 Thomas Aquinas

- Thomas Aquinas (1225 – 7 March 1274)
- Aquinas developed the classical natural law tradition to incorporate Christian theology.
- The grace of God was not in conflict with nor did it abolish human nature, which was intended to perfect. A human, using reason, could participate in the moral order designed by God.
- His order of different kinds of law:

- Eternal law. What is governed by divine reason or Providence.
- Natural law. The participation of humans in ordering the affairs of life by reason, which is involvement in the rational order ordained by God.
- Human law. The particular rules and regulations that humans deduced from the general precepts of natural law, using his reason. Could also be called positive law.
- Divine law. The law revealed by God to man, through scripture or other things. Mostly concerns humans in relation to God and salvation.

4.3 Divine Law, Human Law, and Obligation

- Aquinas took Aristotle's natural law theory and combined it with Christian tradition to develop the most refined theory of natural law before the 20th century.
- Humans, through reason, participates in divine wisdom, the purpose of which is to live in a Christian community.
- Laws will reflect directly or indirectly the universal morality of natural law.
- This theory can be compared to that of Hobbes.
- Natural law (God) lays down two types of guidelines from which humans can reason:
  - *specificatio*: Natural Law says that crimes should be punished, but how?
  - *determinatio*: determination within the boundaries set within the law
- There is an overriding moral requirement to obey the law.

4.4 John Finnis and Modern Natural Law Theory

- John Finnis (28 July 1940 –)
- A student of Hart
- Says that positivism is, at its best, only a partial theory of law; at its worst, a flawed theory.
- He deals with two major arguments against natural law:
  - Moral skepticism (there are no universal moral principles)
    - Moral realists = moral values/principles do exist.
    - Cognitivists = humans can come to know the rules
    - Emotivists = moral beliefs are just expressions of emotional attitudes, and vary
  - The fact/value distinction/the 'naturalistic fallacy' (G.E. Moore)
    - David Hume: one cannot derive an 'ought' from an 'is'
- But Natural Law theory believes there *are* universal principles.
- Finnis says Natural Law theory is founded on man's ability to grasp values directly; it is not necessary to (always) have to infer them.
- There are basic values that exist which humans naturally value. These are:

    1. *life*
    2. *knowledge*
    3. *play*
    4. *aesthetic experience*
    5. *friendship*
    6. *religion*

7. *practical reasonableness.*

- Yet Finnis admits there could be debate his list of seven values.
- Finnis says law is a social institution, which seeks to regulate and create a stable society, where everyone can know these seven values and succeed within them.
- He is not a utilitarian!
- His book, *Natural Law and Natural Rights* (1980, 2011), is a significant contribution to this theory.

4.5 Lon Fuller and Modern Natural Law Theory

- Lon L. Fuller (June 15, 1902 – April 8, 1978)
- Criticized legal positivism.
- Put forth of a theory of a secular natural law theory.
- Did not intend to produce a theory of the morality of law.
  - Instead, he explained that there was a moral content in the concept of 'the rule of law.'
  - This is not a general moral theory, but a theory about the moral aspect of governing by rules.
- His book *The Morality of Law* (1964) addresses these ideas and theories
- As such, his work is often described as a *procedural* natural law theory.
- His 1958 debate with H.L.A. Hart in the *Harvard Law Review* was an important debate between natural law theory and legal positivism

4.6 Summary

- The question of the connection between law and morality is a large and complex area of study.
- Hart, the positivist, was always sensitive to the arguments and tenants of natural law theory, so he often addressed the connections with positivism.
- Ronald Dworkin, who was not a natural law adherent, also saw connections between morality and law, though his was a different approach, and refuted positivism.

5. HLA Hart's: *The Concept of Law*

5.1 Overview

- Hart's attempt to restate the theory of legal positivism for the modern world
- One of the most influential theorists in analytical jurisprudence.
- Published *The Concept of Law* in 1961 to develop his theories of legal positivism (based on a series of 1952 lectures at Harvard Law School.
- He describes what he does as 'descriptive sociology' and 'analytical jurisprudence.'
- For him, the ideal model was the 'modern municipal legal system.'
  - Laws can be identified through the sources of law which are accepted as valid by those under the system.
- Since judges accept the system as a matter of fact, it is not necessary that the law have a moral content. (But it can.)
- Chapters 2-4: Analysis and criticism of Austin and Bentham's Command Theory.
- Chapter 5-6: Hart's main thesis is that law is made up of a union between 'primary' and 'secondary' rules
  - Held together under the 'rule of recognition' (a development from Hans Kelsen's *Grundnorm* concept (see Chapter 10))

- Chapter 9: A defense of legal positivism against possible attacks by natural law theorists.
- Postscript: A reply to Ronald Dworkin's criticism of Hart's theories and is legal positivism in general.

5.2 The Aims of the Theory

- Hart wants to 'produce a descriptive theory of law' by paying attention to legal language as seen in the attitude of people towards law.

5.3 Definition and Theory

- Hart addresses three important questions in his book
    1. What are the differences between law and coercion?
    2. What is the relationship between legal obligation and moral obligation?
    3. What does it mean to say that 'a social rule exists' in a particular society?
- Hart does not believe that "law" can be easily defined because any definition must deal with difficult cases, international law, and primitive law.
- Instead, Hart adopts a 'model' of law, which allows these difficult areas to be held up to the model and compared.
- Hart's model is a central set of elements, a union of primary and secondary rules, that describe the 'modern municipal legal system.'
- This model allows one to posit that international law "is law to the extent that it shares similarities with the model, and not law to the extent that it does not."

5.4 Criticism of the Orders Backed By Threats Theory

- Hart says that social rules involve a standard accepted by at least some members of the group
  - The concept of a rule makes more sense than using the concept of an 'order' (which is hierarchical and a 'one-off').
- When one allows for rules that can refer to legal *duties* and not just standard laws,
  - and also allows for other rules that can refer to powers,
  - it is easy to see how laws apply to the institutions that made them.
  - The Orders Backed By Threats Theory cannot do this easily.
- It also explains why some laws do not appear to have any specific origin (e.g., customary law).

5.5 The 'Union of Primary and Secondary Rules'

- Chapters 5 and 6 of *The Concept of Law* explore Hart's central thesis
  - The 'central set of elements' which constitute law is the 'the union of primary and secondary rules.'
- These rules are
  - duty-imposing rules
  - power-conferring rules
  - and three power-conferring rules
    - rules of change
    - rules of adjudication
    - the rule of recognition.

- These rules describe how legislatures are set up, the public and private powers of legislation, the courts, and criteria of 'legal validity.'
- The rule of recognition, by its nature, is accepted by the judges of the system as a fact.
- To say that any legal system 'exists' means that
  - it is essentially effective
  - the officials of the system accept the rules of recognition which identifies the system as legally valid.

5.6 Legal Reasoning, Natural Law, International Law

- The rest of the chapters are less important to understanding Hart's theories, but provide some background, summaries, and application.
  - Chapter 7: Legal reasoning.
    - Distinguishes between the 'core' and the 'penumbra' in 'settled' law.
    - Critiques American Legal Realism
  - Chapter 8: Discussion of Natural Law
    - Morality and law are connected, but can be distinguished
    - Excellent summary of Natural Law theory
    - Believes that morality is more important in procedural law than in substantive law.
  - Chapter 9: See Chapter 7 of this guide.
  - Chapter 10: Summary and International Law
    - Summarizes his theory regarding the central set of elements

- How this model can account for International law when other theories cannot.

5.7 The 'Internal' Point of View

- The concept of the 'internal point of view' is an important idea in *The Concept of Law* and to Hart's model and theory.
- To Hart, this means that the citizens and official accept the rules of the system *from inside* the system.
  - But he never addresses why anyone would or *should* accept the rule of recognition—they just do.
  - For example, what if a judge in a system took a judicial oath that the only accepted and valid rules had some moral decency (whatever that might mean to them).
  - This would run counter to Hart's theory of legal positivism because the rule of recognition would then have to accept a connection between legal validity and moral decency.
  - Hart makes an *a priori* assumption about the rule of recognition, even though he says he is setting up a stand-alone model based on reason.
- Stephen Perry argued, for this reason, that Hart's methodology is purely neutral and descriptive, as Hart says it is.
  - Hart says he is writing 'descriptive sociology,' but Perry says that Hart is actually evaluation and choosing as he develops his central model of law.
  - Hart is privileging the modern Western legal system, above all others. He loses his claim of a general theory.
  - Hart posits that people regard themselves as under the system, but he never addresses why they do (or why they must).

- His model may require a moral argument, and not just a descriptions, though that is his attempt
- Perry says that an internal account of these things is required to understand the normative activity (the rule-governed nature) of law; otherwise it is not purely descriptive.

6. Hart's Rule of Recognition

6.1 Identifying the Rule

- Hart's 'rule of recognition' functions to identify the law of a particular system.
  - This can be done (according to Hart) by looking at the actual practice of officials in the legal system.
  - Hart calls this the "ultimate rule,"
    - made up of both "supreme" and "subordinate" criteria of legal validity.
- The rule of recognition is also crucial in defining what a legal system is.
  - The 'rule of recognition' identifies whether or not another rule is part of the legal system.
  - The existence of the rule of recognition is simply an empirical fact
  - One determines it by examining the system itself
  - It is often not stated, but can be seen in how particular rules are identified.
- The 'Supreme Criterion' is part of the 'Rule of Recognition' which dominates over the rest of the system.
  - For example, this would be Parliamentary enactments in the UK.

- The ultimate rule is the Rule of Recognition itself, because you cannot go higher in the chain of rules to find the authority for the rule of recognition.
  - It is 'ultimate' in the same sense as Kelsen's *Grundnorm.* (See Chapter 10).
- Austin held that *all* law is the result of legislation, Hart points to the distinction between the Supreme Criterion and Rule of Recognition to show this is a flawed view.

The Validity of a Legal System

- Officials in the system accept the Rule of Recognition
  - It is not necessary that private citizens have this 'internal attitude' towards it.
- But valid legal rules are generally obeyed by both officials and private citizens.

6.2 Criticisms

- Finnis criticizes Hart's rule of recognition
  - He says it places too much emphasis on its identification through empirical fact—surely some evaluative criteria are required?
  - if a moral evaluation (that, for example, the Rule of Recognition must serve some moral function such as enabling us to lead our lives in a better way) is required, then there *will* be a "necessary" link between law and morality.
- Dworkin criticizes the Rule of Recognition because it leaves judicial reasoning outside of law

- Since legal reasoning in hard cases is controversial, the Rule of Recognition cannot adequately justify the law to be applied.
- Finnis, in *Natural Law and Natural Rights*
  - Hart never describes with specifics how officials are to view the Rule of Recognition.
  - There must be a central set of elements (according to Hart's own definitional technique!)
  - Finnis believes there must be a *moral* acceptance of the rule.
  - (McCormick makes similar criticism).
- Dworkin, *Taking Rights Seriously*:
  - The purpose of Rule of Recognition is to 'cure the defect of uncertainty' in a society that only has primary rules.
    - This means that any rule which cannot be identified with certainty is not a rule of law at all.
  - Therefore, says Dworkin, the hard cases, where it is difficult to identify a rule with certainty, are not concerned with law (according to Hart). In other words, if it is controversial, it is not a law:
    - So a judge must then legislate (create a new rule to deal with the hard case)
    - When the judge applies this new rule, it is retrospective legislation, which is unfair and not how we think judges act!
    - Therefore, Dworkin says, Hart's is misdescribing what judges do and say they do (because most judges would say they are 'finding' or 'interpreting' law rather than legislating).
    - Because a major part of the law involves legal *argument*, positivism fails as a model.

  - One could defend Hart by pointing out that he did distinguish between 'core' meanings and 'penumbras' of the rules.
  - Dworkin says that clear meanings are only clear because of some interpretation made
    - Example: s.51 Adoption Act 1951; *R v Registrar of Births* 1991
- Finnis' and Dworkin's arguments have the following in common:
  - a proper legal theory must explain the moral force of law;
  - the proper operation of law requires making the best *moral* sense of the existing legal practices.

6.3 The Postscript

- Hart repeats the line that is apparent in the early part of *The Concept of Law*:
  - Legal theory involves a descriptive account of the concept of law.
- He denies that legal theory is interested in justification, and distinguishes himself from Dworkin on this ground. Hart is only describing.
- He reaffirms that evil legal systems are as much law as moral legal systems.

The Hart and Dworkin Debate

- The postscript is Hart's counter to Dworkin's attack on legal positivism.
- Hart says his theory is both descriptive *and* general, and that he is addressing no particular legal system.

  - It is morally neutral and makes no justifications about any of it.
  - This is very different than what Dworkin does:
    - attempts evaluate and justify
    - addresses a particular legal system.
- Hart takes exception being guilty of the "semantic sting" (no sound theory of law can be based purely on how people speak about it).
  - Argues that he has no such theory
    - Yet chapters 1-4 seem to do exactly that
    - By the end of book, Hart *has* made choices between differing theories and concepts (see Ch 9).
- Hart does not believe that the point or purpose of law is to justify coercion.
- He argues that the Nazi legal system was still valid law, regardless of how morally bankrupt, because of the features it shares with modern municipal legal systems
- In sum, Hart says he concerned about *universal* descriptions while Dworkin is about *justification* of a state's coercive powers
  - Therefore they are talking about two different things (when it comes to the Nazi legal system).

Principles and the Rule of Recognition

- Hart believes Dworkin makes too sharp a distinction between rules and principles.
- Believes that Dworkin is wrong about *Riggs v Palmer*
  - It is *not* a clash between two principles, but between a rule and a principle.

Judicial Discretion

- Dworkin thinks that judicial law-making is a threat to democracy; Hart does not
  - Hart does not seem to make much of any distinction in the roles of the executive and judiciary, which is emphasized in Western democracies. (see quote of p 275 of *The Concept of Law*).
- Hart says the application of retrospective legislation in hard cases doesn't matter because:
  - Anyone surprised by a judge's application of retrospective law would also be surprised that there was a law already there.
  - Yet the defendant is worse off in when the law operates retrospectively, because of the principle of *nulla poena sine lege*. (which Hart invokes in Chapter 9!)

7. Hart's Defenses Against Natural Law Theorists and Fuller

7.1 Morality

- Hart believes that American Realist adherents are wrong when they argue that morality becomes part of law when judges make decisions.
- Hart has no problem admitting that this does sometimes happen, but not always, and it does not have to.
- He points out that, just as easily, immorality could come into the law in the same way.

7.2 The Nazi Grudge Informer

- The "Nazi Grudge Informer"
  - Where a citizen, under the laws of the time, informs on another citizen (perhaps they disparaged Hitler, which was illegal at the time).
  - These citizens were not *required* to report someone, but they could, and so might do so to "get back" at the offender for some personal reason (thus, "grudge" informer.)
  - The offending citizen is arrested, tortured, put to death, or sent to the front lines of the war.

  - After the fall of the Nazi regime, some of these 'informers' were persecuted under an 1871 German law that made it an offense to "illegally depriving a person of his freedom."
  - These defendants argued that their actions were legal under Nazi laws, and therefore should not be prosecuted.
- Legal Positivism would argue that the grudge informer acted legally, though also immorally.
- Natural Law theory would argue that just because that the action was immoral does not mean there is a legal defense, because the Nazi law itself was immoral (against nature) and so invalid.
- Hart argues that positivism makes more sense of the situation because it gives the grudge informer a legal defense.
  - If the defense is weak when compared with moral requirements, then the informer would need to be punished.
  - A retrospective law is the only way to negate the defense.
- Hart sees the advantage here is that this view can demonstrate that the rule of law is being violated by doing what is morally right.
- This suggests that Hart thinks Positivism is justified in practice because it results in a morally better result than natural law theory would.
  - If so, then Hart contradicts his argument that there is no moral bias in his theory.

7.3 Fuller's Principles of the 'Inner Morality' of the Law

- Fuller believes that evil endeavors do not operate logically, but moral endeavors do.
- Therefore, if law can be logically and rationally structured regarding principles, it can be moral, too.

- The principles of the 'inner morality of law' are that they should
  1. be promulgated
  2. not be retroactive
  3. be general
  4. be clear
  5. not be inconsistent
  6. not require the impossible
  7. be congruent with official action
  8. be reasonably stable
- Hart's criticism of these eight principles is that it is easy to come up with 'eight principles' of anything, even immoral acts: "we could just as easily have eight principles of inner morality of the poisoner's art," or Naziism, or of playing chess.
- It can be argued that this criticism misses morally serious nature of claims made by appealing to "the law."

8. Raz's Theory of Law: Service Conception

8.1 The Paradox of Authority and the 'Service' Conception of Authority

- The 'paradox of authority' refers to the concept that it makes no sense to follow authority:
  - if an authority tells you what to do or think, then you should do it because it is the right thing to do or think, not because authority told you to.
  - If an authority tells you to do something that is not right, then you should not do it.
  - Therefore, the authority telling you to do something makes no difference.
  - Those who subscribe to this concept are called 'philosophical anarchists.'
- The argument against the paradox is that society would be worse off if there were no authority, which provides a structure to society and sets norms.
- Hobbes believed that the legitimacy of a state was found in a 'social contract' between all citizens (including leaders).
- Others argue that because authorities spend their time thinking about laws (enacting or carrying out) they know more than a regular citizen does

  - Example: a person listens to a medical doctor as an authority because the doctor knows medicine, and knows how to understand your vital signs.
- Joseph Raz (21 March 1939–) calls this the 'service conception' of authority.

8.2 *The 'Normal Justification Theory'*

- Raz's 'normal justification' theory addresses the authority paradox.
- It is rational to follow authority if the authority understands the reasons behind the rules which apply to you.

The Balance of Reasons

- Raz suggests one reason for this is because of the 'balance of reasons.'
- When you choose to go to a doctor rather than diagnose and treat yourself, you are balancing:
  - your financial situation (because you have to pay the doctor)
  - You could learn medicine yourself, but that takes time away from your life and making money.
  - Remaining healthy is important to keep working, making money so that you can live.
- An authority (such as a doctor) serves you ('service conception') by helping you balance the reasons.

The Normal Justification Thesis

- Legal authorities mediates this balance in your life in much the same way a doctor does:

  - The doctor does not train you in medicine, but gives you a prescription/operation/course of action.
- A legislature considers and debates reasons and purposes, then passes a law.
- Authority gains legitimacy when it mediates these issues that apply to you, and does the work (so you don't have to) in a way that helps you and society.

The Scope of Authority

- The law has more justified authority over some areas than others.
- Some see this as a flaw in Raz's theory because the law *claims* equal authority over all areas of its subject matter.

8.3 Exclusionary Reasons

-Authorities do their work in two stages:

- Deliberative Reasoning: the debates, research, nd discussions that lead to a rule or law being passed.
  - Executive Reasoning: the stage at which that decision is implemented.
- Decision-making bodies are authorities
  - the results of their debates and discussions are taken as exclusionary reasons
  - their work is intended to govern the citizens over which they have authority.
- Raz argues that this demonstrates that authorities are an important part of practical reasoning.

- Orders made by authorities are meaningful because they have thought through the 'balance of reasons'.
  - Those deliberations also limit the scope.
  - But these orders can lose that exclusionary force if the procedure of deliberation has faults or errors.
- deliberative and the executive phases.
  - When a person chooses to follow an order of an authority (rather than their own balancing of reasons), this imparts exclusionary reason to the authority.
  - The person is now relying on the authorities, and *not* on acting on their own 'balance of reasons'.
  - This allows deliberative and executive stages of practical reasoning to be employed for difference situations and to different groups of people.
  - When the deliberative part is done (lawmaking in a legislature, judge and lawyers arguing a case), and we enter the executive phase, the citizens must follow.

Force and Scope of the Reasons

- 'Exclusionary reasons' replace reasons that any person might come to on their own by balancing of reasons.
  - They do not add to the balance of reasons, they stand on their own (as authoritative).
- Exclusionary reasons are about actions, not thinking about them.
- Opposition parties have a right to continue their criticism of a law after the executive stage, but would rarely suggest ignoring the law because they believe it wrong.
- Exclusionary reasons have scope.

  - This scope does not extend to issues or reasons that were not addressed in the deliberative stage.
  - If new evidence arose that suggests a change in the law might be in order (judge drunk, error in evidence, etc.), this could lead to new deliberation and change.

8.4 The Authority and Scope of Law

- The law claims the authority to make rules
- The expects people to follow the rules.
  - Whether people believe the law is just or unjust is irrelevant to their following the law.
- Raz's theory says that the law mediates between the balance of reasons and it citizens.
  - It is limited by the scope of what makes some person or group an authority.
  - Raz also argues that any particular point of law cannot depend on moral arguments for its reasons.
- The process of the making of authoritative laws:
  - An authority has authority because it can mediate between balance of reasons for its citizens
  - It deliberates and then issues an order (law, ruling).
  - The order cannot be authoritative if it does not mediate between the balance of reasons (if it leaves that to the people).
  - The orders must be specific enough to give direction
    - If someone has to figure out what the law requires, it is not authoritative.

    - Yet there are directives of this kind: a law or regulation that requires individuals to act with 'fairness and reasonableness' in certain circumstances. ('Good faith,' 'reasonable accommodations,' etc.)
  - If the order is not specific, then it cannot be ordered.
    - The law is not authoritative if it makes orders that require more delibcration.
    - Because the authority proceeded to the executive stage without completing the deliberative stage, it does not possess genuine authority.

8.5 Soft Positivism

- An order has authority if it is possible to follow it
  - on its own terms
  - without the need for further deliberation about the problem that the order intended to address.
- Raz argues that laws which refer to anything 'morality requires' are not authoritative orders
  - Because they require people under the law to 'solve the problem' by weighing moral reasons
  - The authority is supposed to mediate these deliberations themselves because they are in a better placed to do so.
- Therefore, argues Raz, laws which refer to 'what morality requires' are really orders that give judges the power to:
  - make specific orders in specific cases
  - create laws or orders which can be followed by people without further deliberation.
- All legal systems seem to contain laws of this kind, therefore, all legal systems give judges this power

– This argument supports Hart's claim that judges do have the authority to sometimes make law.

– Dworkin disagrees

9. Practical Reason and the Law

9.1 Definitions

- Norm: A standard of behavior or action considered 'normal' or 'proper' for a given group or society. A measure against which actions can be assessed.
- Rule: A general directive that applies in more than once situation or circumstance.
- Order: A one-time norm which guides the behavior or actions of an individual or group.
- Rights: a way of expressing norms from the perspective of a given individual.
  - Rights correlate with duties.
  - Some rights can be exercised (liberties)
  - Other rights give entitlement, but do not require an exercise of the right.
- Powers: A normative capacity to create, alter, or abolish other norms.
- Duties: exclusionary reasons (in Raz's terms).
  - They can correlate to rights or can be rules

9.2 Norms

- Norms are the standards of behavior that people are expected to follow.
- Rules, rights, duties, and powers are types of norms, written or promulgated in different ways.
- Rights can be
  - general (for everyone)
    - *in rem*, rights governs the behavior of everyone
  - specific (for certain people or groups)
    - *in personam*, which binds only a specified individual or individuals
- The "choice" or "will" theory of rights says that rights are ones in which the rights-holder can choose to exercise them (or not).
- The "interest" theory of rights (more in favor at present), focuses on the inherent nature of the right, which protects the interests of rights-holders, regardless of whether the rights-holder chooses to exercise them or not.

9.3 Hohfeld's Theory of Legal Norms

- Wesley Newcomb Hohfeld (8 August 1879 – 21 October 1918)
  - Followed early American Realist theories
- Theory focuses on what courts do
  - Each right corresponds to a duty
  - Each power corresponds to a liability
  - Distinguishing claim rights from liberties, powers, and immunities.

- Some argue that the scheme does not really reflect how these concepts work out in the legal field.
- For example, it may not make sense to say that liberty rights cannot correlate with duties.

9.4 Rule-Following

- Hart's practical theory of rules says that a rule exists if there is a practice of acting on it, and that breaking it causes a response. This theory is criticized for:
  - for not making a distinction between rules and reasons that are generally accepted
  - for not being able to define the normativity of rules, which does not depend on a practice of them.
- Wittgenstein's argument about rule-following denies that rules are standards dictated by past precedents or by clear formulations of what a rule requires
  - Rather, he argues, people follow rules and their deviations because they share an understanding the context in the culture, and the purpose of the rules.
- Rules can be revised or negated when they are not applicable in situations outside the purpose of them which.

9.5 Hard Cases

- If a law leads to an unjust or harsh result, then that was not the purpose, and in these cases, rules are defeasible.
  - The classical concept of 'equity' is often applied in such cases;

  - but are also the reason for the classic saying, “hard cases make bad law.”
- If the specific situation requires a difficult judgment in its application of a law.
  - This is often the case when subjective concepts of law must be employed (i.e., ‘reasonableness’’; see Dworkin's discussion of *Bolton v Stone*).
- If two or more laws conflict
  - See *Midland Bank v Green* 1981. Such cases make the saying “Like cases should be decided alike” difficult to apply
  - See also *Donaghue v Stevenson.*
- If two or more difficult laws could reasonably underlie a series of cases or a statute.
- Rules can be interpreted in different ways by different judges.
  - Often because of uncertainty in the scope of a law, often seen in complex systems with statutes.

10. Kelsen's Theory of Law: Norms and Delicts

10.1 Overview

– Hans Kelsen (October 11, 1881 – April 19, 1973)

– Represents a continental form of Legal Positivism.

– Believed law could be identified purely by its form rather than content

  – Therefore, he called his theory of law a 'pure' theory of law.

– The task is to define action-directing rules of behavior (norms) which either places duties on people or give them powers.

  – This is an objective task.

  – Morality is a subjective opinion.

– Reading and understanding Kelsen can be difficult because

  – it is a translation of the original German

  – It makes use of German philosophical terms.

– An important term is the *Grundnorm*, which is the assumption by which laws are considered valid.

10.2 The **Grundnorm** *and Delicts*

– Kelsen's theory takes the point of view of those in power.

- Citizen commit 'delicts', which is not disobeying the law, because the law is directed at officials, not citizens.
- Officials are to apply sanctions when a delict is committed: the law tells them when and how
- All valid laws rest on a higher norm or law, eventually reaching the the *Grundnorm* , which is based on the assumption that it is valid.
- This is different than Austin's and Hart's, who argue that validity is based on facts, not an assumption of validity.
- But Kelson also argues that the effectiveness of a system is a necessary condition for any system.

The Legal Norm

- Law is the means used to 'order human behaviour' which 'designates a specific technique of social organisation'.
- The system gives the power to authorities to use sanctions in certain situations and times.
- 'Coercion' and 'officialdom' concept are common to all systems of law.
- A 'legal norm' is a rule that requires an authority to enforce a sanction in certain situations at certain times.
- An argument against Kelsen's view is that most people think law is directed at the citizens, not the people who enforce the laws.

The Delict

- According to Kelsen, laws are directed at the authorities, not directed at citizens
  - When a citizen does something that should cause an authority to apply a sanction, he or she has committed a 'delict'.

- Kelsen says there is no reason to make reference to law in such a situation, because the law is not directed at the citizen (it is not a norm).
  - Instead, the concept is that, 'if someone commits a delict, then the official should impose the relevant sanction.
- Yet Kelsen says it is easier to think of laws as directed at citizens, despite the fact that it is not a norm.
- Because the action of a delict by a citizen only places an obligation on the authority, only officials can break the law.

The Basic Norm (the ***Grundnorm)***

- As one moves up the chain of validity of each law, the highest law is the ultimate norm
  - This is the one that gives validity to all others.
  - For example, a law in the UK can be traced up the chain of validity, until reaching the 'Crown-in-Parliament'.
  - There is no higher authority to confer validity.
  - Why is the Crown-in-Parliament the ultimate norm? Kelsen would say it is the ultimate norm because it is assumed so by the system.

Austin

- Kelsen believes his theory is more sound than that of Austin because a norm is more like a rule than it is like a command.
- Kelsen's believes his idea of a norm works better because it can distinguish between 'being obliged' from being 'under obligation' which Austin's theory cannot do ('Orders Backed By Threats')

- Kelsen's *Grundnorm* is the ultimate validity of a system, another norm, which he believes makes more sense than resting it on a person or a group in Austin's theory (the habitually-obeyed 'sovereign')

Hart

- Kelsen's basic norm is a presupposition of the ultimate authority, rather than a matter of fact as in Hart's theory.
- This means that the presupposition of a revolution regime could simply be ignored (refuse to suppose it), which could not take place in Hart's theory (if it was habitually obeyed after a time).
- The basic norm relies on the concept that authorities act under the first constitution of a system, which was made authoritative at some point in history (think of the US Constitution)
  - It is not a *fact* of the first constitution, as Hart would say, it is the presupposed norm.
- Importantly, Kelsen says that effectiveness is not a *sufficient condition* for the validity, but it is a *necessary* condition. Hart believes it is sufficient.

10.3 Legal Revolutions

- In the Kelsen system, a full-scale revolution where a new government introduced a new constitution that did not match the old would have the following issues with legitimacy:
  - It would need to be effective.
  - All the old laws would not longer be valid because the basic norm is no longer presupposed.
  - But a new regime is not automatically valid.
  - It is *effective* but not yet *sufficient*

- Some old laws might still be valid, which would make it still the presupposed norm.

Theory of Revolution in the Real World

- *State v Dosso PLD* (Pakistan Legal Decisions) 1958
  - 1958, Pres of Pakistan issued proclamation that the 1956 Constitution was null and void
  - He dismissed cabinet and dissolved Parliament
  - Ordered that all laws, except the 1956 Constitution, were still valid.
  - The Chief Justice ruled that this new regime was valid because it was effective (that is, the revolution had been successful).
  - He based thus ruling on Kelsen's theory, but he was reading Kelsen as if he had said 'success' meant 'validity.'
- A similar situation occurred eight years later in *Uganda v The Commissioner of Prisons, ex parte Matovu* [1966] with a similar decision.
- In Rhodesia, a third similar situation was addressed in *Madzimbamuto v Lardner-Burke* [1966]
  - The judges held that the revolutionary government was not valid
  - But they recognized the actions of the new governments as enforceable on the 'principle of necessity' (because someone had to govern)
  - Eventually, the Rhodesian court accepted that the illegal government had become legal through effectiveness. *R v Ndhlovu* 1968
- In *Dosso* and *Uganda* decisions, each court had to decide the question of fact: was the new government in control?

- Each court referred to Kelsen's 'doctrine of effectiveness' as if the *fact* of effectiveness was enough for legal validation.
- But Kelson had theorized that effectiveness is necessary but not sufficient! (a regime could be effective and still not sufficient).

10.4 Criticisms

- He places civil and criminal law together as one, which is not how they work in most jurisdictions.
- All laws are directed at officials: this is not how most people understand how the law works.
- Most people do not think of their system of law changing every time there is a change that does not fall under the presupposed norm (constitution).
  - For example, the UK and NZ have separate legal systems, get the validity of the NZ system were given by a law of the UK.
  - Some argue that the concept of *Grundnorm* can help define different legal systems, but the above case it does not
- Raz does not believe that Kelsen's 'justified normatively' approach works.
  - It is normative because some people (authorities?) say it is. That is an issue of fact, not a presupposition.
  - For Raz, this is like saying the system is authoritative because it is made up of rules
- Hart makes the same point in *The Concept of Law*:
  - 'To express this simple fact by saying darkly that its validity is "assumed but cannot be demonstrated", is like saying that we assume, but can never demonstrate, that the standard metre bar in Paris which is the ultimate test of the correctness of all measurement of metres, is itself correct.'

11. Dworkin's Theory of Law

Ronald L. Dworkin (December 11, 1931 – February 14, 2013)

11.1 Interpretation and Practice

- Dworkin's believes law is best understood through its practice.
- The theorist job is to figure out what would be the best sense of that practice
- Dworkin calls this 'constructive' or 'artistic interpretation'.
  - not 'scientific interpretation' which interprets things
  - not 'conversational interpretation' which interprets what people mean.
- If a legal practice is understood in its best light, and there seems to be no purpose or point to it, then it should probably be abolished.

Definition of 'Interpretation'

- The work of Dworkin's theory is to describe a legal practice 'at its best'.
- To put it 'in its best light'.
- The theorist will assume that it has a purpose.

- Dworkin contrasts what he does with constructive/artistic interpretation (which tries to interpret things created by people as separate from the practice or the people)

Types of Attitudes Towards the Law

- He defines practices that have point or purpose, cultural customs, as *pre-interpretive* (his example is 'men doffing hats to women').
- The *interpretive* task asks for reasons for a practice; it can have different interpretations applied to it by different people, that is, it creates arguments about the practice
- A *Post-Interpretive* approach to interpretation of something 'folds back on itself', that is, the thing changes because of a different perception of it.
- Thus Dworkin believes there is a much more to a rule than simply being able to describe it.

11.2 Judge Hercules

- Dworkin posits a fictional judge whom he called 'Judge Hercules' to help explain his theory
- Some have criticized the technique by saying no such judges exists, but this misses the purpose of using a fiction character!
- Hercules the model an *ideal* judge, who works within the system at its best and at his best.
- Hercules is a model against which good and bad legal arguments can then be judged.
- Since his theory is based on the argumentative nature of the legal system, it requires this 'best practice' model against which to measure it.

- Hercules is a judge who accepts the settled practice and general political theory of the legal system he is a part of.
- In hard cases, he accepts and employs the settled rules
- Because he understands settled practice and the political theory, he understands the theories that support the rules. Dworkin gives the following common examples:
  - theory of responsibility in criminal law (*mens rea*, recklessness)
  - theory of relevance in law of evidence
  - theory of division of capital and income in law of taxation
  - theory of consideration in law of contract

11.3 Principles and Policies

- Dworkin believes that arguments about principles are arguments about rights.
- Arguments about legal policy are about reaching the goals a community sets for itself.
- For Dworkin, these two areas are crucial to distinguish because
  - they are distinctions drawn by lawyers (descriptive)
  - It defines the separation between what is legitimate for judges and a state to do, and follow the standard 'separation of powers' doctrine.
- It is in these areas where Dworkin's attacks Utilitarianism.

11.4 'Fit' and 'Substance'.

- Hercules illustrates what the best judicial decision-making would look like based on his acceptance of settled rules and policy.
- For example, judges would not attempt to legislate because
  - judges are elected (or appointed) to represent the community; they are not elected as lawmakers
  - judges should only be dealing with rights principles, not policy issues (because those are for community goals).
- Therefore, a judge's decisions should be in concert with present, accepted, received law
  - In difficult cases, where there are conflicts of these laws, a judge should attempt to resolve in in a way that results in 'equality of respect' for the most people.

Example of *McLoughlin v O'Brien*

- Dworkin uses this case to illustrate his theory and practice
- Facts: Husband and children in car accident; the wife went to hospital and was told that a daughter was dead and husband and other children seriously injured; the wife suffered severe shock and sued driver and others for it
- Dworkin suggested six possible ways to interpret and apply settled rules:
  - Liable only where physical injury (the facts do not fit the law of tort)
  - Emotional injury can only occur at the accident (the settled rules draw an arbitrary and necessary moral line)

- Economically efficient (this is a policy a government, not a principle, so Dworkin rules this out as irrelevant to the plaintiff's rights)
- Where the injury was a direct consequence of accident (but this contradicts the principle of foreseeability)
- Where the injury is foreseeable (Dworkin thinks this is one of two best options)
- Where the injury is foreseeable, except when it would place an unfair financial burden on the defendant (Dworkin thinks this is one of two best options)

11.5 Concepts, Conceptions, Argumentation

- Dworkin's uses the distinction between conceptions and concepts along with his interpretive approach to critique other legal theories.
  - Pragmatism cannot address or make sense of principles or rights.
  - Conventionalism cannot produce an adequate account of the community or its goals.
- 'Integrity' makes the best sense:
  - it accounts for rights
  - it can unite the community
  - allows for a full and complete account of legal reasoning.

Skepticism and Truth

- Dworkin notes that a significant challenge to any interpretation that seeks 'truth' has to deal with issues of opinion (because they cannot be proved)

- If one looks at the law with a skeptical approach (what Dworkin calls 'global internal skepticism') one must be skeptical of the theories of interpretation of law
- He notes that 'external' skepticism is not engaged in the system, and therefore pointless in this endeavor.
- Dworkin believes that law exists to restrain government, for which he says there are three approaches:
  - Conventionalism. This method makes the law more predictable for judges and parties and results in procedural fairness
  - Pragmatism is always looking at the future and therefore is a skeptical approach.
  - Integrity. This approach both ensures quality of procedure and application among all citizens, and therefore makes the community more genuine.
- Dworkin stresses that the relationship between law and morality is not merely semantic, it is interpretative.
  - Example: Nazi laws could be considered 'law' if it could be analyzed as a fully developed legal system. This would require a moral content in Dworkin's view.

The Argumentative Attitude

- Dworkin argues that law is not just a bunch of rules, it is an attitude.
- This is seen in the courtroom as lawyers make arguments—this is an attitude towards an end and a goal larger than just the case at hand.

11.6 The 'One Right Answer' Thesis

- Some think that the proper theory, applied correctly, could result in the right answer in every instance.
- Dworkin does not have such a theory (though some accuse him of trying to develop one)
  - Dworkin argues that everyone believes there are right answers to issues, even if they can't be proved.
- Even if someone denies a 'one right answer' thesis, they believe *that* to be true, and so are contradicting their own view.

11.7 Evil Legal Systems

- When it comes to the discussion of 'evil' legal systems, Dworkin makes distinction between:
  - The ground of law, which means analyzing and interpreting the practices of a system from within that system (like Hercules does)
    - With this approach, one could claim Nazi law is law.
  - The moral force of the law.
    - For Dworkin, this is the second necessary step in discussing such systems of law
    - He says that many theories fail because the theorists stop at the first step (the ground of law) and do no proceed to look then at the moral force of the law they are examining.
- Hart and others say that with this way of thinking, Dworkin is merely adding to positivism or coming up with a 'confused' version.
- Dworkin's argument against this is complex:

- Part of the problem is that there are times where a citizen does have a duty to obey a law, even though he or she may think it is a morally bad law.
- If Dworkin is arguing that some moral judgments are addressing whether a State has a right or duty to use its coercive powers, then one could say he is using Natural Law theory.
- If he believes that moral systems are not law, then he cannot be following Natural Law theory.
- On the other hand, if he is only saying that there are some natural answers that can lead us to have some objectivity in making both moral and legal arguments, then he cannot be following Natural Law.

11.8 Hart's Postscript

- Dworkin believes there *are* right answers to both legal and moral questions
  - He believes this because he says that's what lawyers (and everyone) do—argue and analyze to make those decisions.
- He argues that, since evil legal systems and moral systems share common characteristics, that
  - it makes no sense to say, without a doubt, that evil legal systems cannot be 'law'.
  - Yet he also notes that evil systems lack a moral justification to carry out legitimate coercive acts.
- Dworkin cannot be following natural law, because he never argues that reaching the model answer means finding a natural morality.
  - He also believes that evil legal systems *do* exist.
- Because of this, some accuse him of being a sort of positivist, but Dworkin argues that he is not.

  - Hart's claims (in his Postscript) to have found the concept of law
  - Raz's claims that law is identified by a social source alone
- Dworkin argues that without locating the *point* of finding law with a social source, it is not possible to find that source.
  - It cannot be identified by determining the meanings of words, since people can disagree about those definitions
  - It cannot be identified by finding some common element (like a DNA match), because there is obviously not one for law.
  - Neither Hart or Raz can be making empirical generalizations about law, because they do not present any empirical evidence.
- Hart's claims that moral principles *can* be part of the law (this is called 'soft positivism') would mean that one has to make moral judgments when defining and analysis get the law, and this is contrary to what Hart's arguments about legal positivism.
- Dworkin presents three ways in which a legal theory might be called descriptive:
  - It could be a semantic description.
  - It could employ a natural kind or type for law (as in science)
  - It could do as Hart does by attempting an empirical generalization
- 'Soft positivists' see social sources as the best way to identifying law (as opposed to Rax and 'hard' or 'exclusive' positivism).
  - In this approach, one must make a moral judgment to identify legal rules as defined by those social sources.
  - Example: In the US, the Eighth Amendment contains a prohibition against 'cruel and unusual punishment.' Any lack of clarity in applying this rule can be made by making a moral judgment based on what the social sources would require.

- Dworkin argues that this approach is hollow because:
  - It says that 'judges should decide cases in the manner that judges should decide cases.'
  - It is wrong because it makes the assumption that there are conventions among judges as to how they will decide such cases—there are not.
- Dworkin also argues that it is not clear how legal positivist can:
  - Make the assumption that propositions about the sources theory are somehow different from other kinds of propositions about the law.
- Dworkin characterizes that the approach of legal positivism as descriptive, even though they deny it.

12. Marxism and Marxist Legal Theory

12.1 Ideology, Economy, and Society

- Karl Marx (5 May 1818 – 14 March 1883)
- Marx developed his theory of society and law through his analysis and critiques of Martin Hegel's theories.
  - Hegel's writings were an overarching analysis of human history and human societal development, which Hegel saw as moving the growth in a positive, progressive direction.
- Marx disagreed with Hegel's idealistic view
  - He especially took exception with the view that the state of Prussia was the view that the apogee of history.
  - Instead, Marx used a materialistic understanding of social institutions (like law) as a way to understand the social economic context of them.

- Marxism later became a political ideology that and movement.

Marx and Hegel

- Marx was a philosopher and stands in a long line of philosophers who react, develop, and argue against one another's concepts.
- Marx believed that law was not part of philosophy that examined the 'development of the human mind'.

- Instead, law should be examined in terms of the 'material conditions of life' (which Hegel referred to as 'civil society')
  - This is Marx's way of discussing the economy of a society.
- Marx's theories were larger than just law—he saw law as only one part of the social and political structure of a society.
- Therefore, if one wanted to understand society, one must examine and understand its economic organization.
  - The 'means of production' was Marx's term for this structure (which encompassed production, distribution, and exchange).
- The 'sense of self' which any one person (or level of society) possesses comes from their material position in society (peasant, landowner, etc.)
- The ideology of each group will determine what they believe about their role, their society, and their values, in a sort of mystical way.
  - For example, a peasant will accept the authority of the lord as 'the way things are', but will not realize that this belief only exists because the lord is the one with wealth and power.
- By viewing 'law' as part of this whole system, its independence can be taken away.
  - Then one can see it for what it is: an instrument of class power.
- Marx defended the 'base' (or foundation) of society that which can be determined by looking at the mode of production, the organization of the economy, and all social institutions.

Marx's Critique of Hegel

- Hegel found that the law was located in history and social experience

  - the law develops through dealing with and resolving contradictions in the system
  - Hegel's system was that law supersedes morality, moral affects families, families affect the larger society, and the larger social affect world history.
- Marx thought this was wrong: the division of labor and classes is not developed through legislation of those with power to do so; it comes from the conditions of material production.

Marx's Contribution

- Not all states are built on the concept and ground of private property
- Law is not one thing that stands above or apart others' it is part of a larger system
- The Prussian state of the time was not the same as the Roman Republic, Roman Empire, or that of early German communities.
- The form of law in any given system is determined by its historical and material circumstances.
- Law is not grounded in legislative rules, but the conditions of material production
- Marx describes how capital takes on a judicial form, which changes over time as society and those in power change.

12.2 Theory of the State

- Those who own property control the State
  - (Marx called this class the 'bourgeoisie')
- These property owners become organized and a political group and take control of the State.

- Because the State is in control of that class, and that class acts in their best interest, the State (and law) reflects the best interest of that class.
  - Therefore, justice and equality will reflect the interests of that class and not some idealistic view of 'justice' and 'equality'.
- Marx's theory sees legal theory as an expression of class power.

12.3 Theory of Law

- *Das Kapital* is Marx's complex discuss of this social and economic theory, part of which is his theory of law
  - What law looks like is determined by the economic interests of those in power.
  - Those in power use the system to exploit those the other classes.
  - Marx argued that if those who are being exploited could organize themselves, they might be able to turn the law to work for them.
  - But real social justice comes only through a transformation of the economic system.
- The movement to regulate the working day in the 19th century was fostered by class interests and struggles.
  - Technology offers the possibility of increased productivity
  - This favors an unregulated work day (for example, it could allow the mill and factory owners to determine what the work day should look like)
  - It would be in their interests to increase the work day, to increase production.
  - This resulted in calls to regulate how long an employee can be required to work in one day.

- The legal system and its laws attempted (and still attempt) to keep up with changes in society and technology social.
- The changes in technology forced many industries to re-organize how they think and operate.
  - In turn, the law was required to change the definition a 'factory' to include 'any place where work is done'.
- Marx argued, then, that the creation of the 'normal' working day is actually the result of a 'civil war' between the capitalist class and the working-class
  - Marx is critical of the law's ability to bring about social justice.
  - It could only happen by those who are exploited coming together and engaging in a civil war to bring about social change.
    - He believes that trade unions would not be able to accomplish such a change, in spite of their protection of the exploited workers.
    - Instead, the prevailing economic order and the State (and its laws) must be overthrown.
    - Therefore, social justice could only be achieved through a revolution.

12.4 Soviet Marxism

- The Russian Revolution of 1917 is a critical historical development of Marxist thought.
- If one views the Revolution as successful, then the later problems and dissolution of the Soviet Union means there was something incorrect about Marxism, or that it was applied incorrectly.

- Vladimir Lenin (1870–1924) wrote that if Marx was correct, and the State acts in the interest of the ruling class, then a revolution is necessary to destroy that State and replace it with a socialist State.
  - The laws set up by the bourgeoisie must be destroyed where it relates to ownership of private property.
  - Lenin's approach is more gradual than an outright revolution and overthrown.
- Evgeny Pashukanis (1891–1937)
  - A famous Soviet legal theorist and writer.
  - He argued for
    - A planned economy
    - The destruction of private property
  - He said that the result of this is that law would cease to function.
  - He also contrasted capitalism with feudalism
  - One of the major criticisms of his theory is that it has no answer to how law could operate in a society with no market economy.
  - Without an answer to this question, the Soviet version of Marxism would seem to be a failure.

12.5 Western Marxism

- Louis Pierre Althusser (16 October 1918 – 22 October 1990)
- Used Marx's theories to relate a person as a social being and how they relate to the economy.

- This view was a more sophisticated theory than Marx's, which was severely deterministic in the relations and influence between the economic base and the social ideologies.

12.6 Marxism and International Law

- Modern theories that who have attempted to apply Marxist theories to a global economy have focused on issues of class and larger global power structures.
- Paul Alexander Baran (1909–1964)
  - Examined how wealth was transferred from the colonized nations and the Commonwealth to Western European nations.
  - He argued that the main reason for the growth of industrial development in First-World Nations was akin to the peasant and the landlord—the agricultural nations were forced to serve the developed economies of the 'colonial masters'.
- Immanuel Maurice Wallerstein (1930–)
  - Known for developing what he called a ‘worlds systems theory’
  - Argued that the world economy should be viewed as a result of the geographic expansions of Western countries beginning in the 16th century.
- Others argue that the concepts of social justice on an international scale should not be the focus of law; it is too narrow a way to regulate global markets.

13. Liberalism

13.1 Utilitarian Approach

- Utilitarianism is a moral theory
- Bentham was the first to write extensively about it.
- The theory had a major effect on the growth of English and Commonwealth society, the growth of liberalism, and current economics practices and theory.
- Utilitarianism is a theory that encompasses more than law
- It is not one theory; there are many variations.
- Adherents of Utilitarianism often complain that those who criticize it do not realize its ability is that critics misunderstand how refined its application can be.
  - For example, 'rule utilitarianism' defends itself against those who would criticize it by pointing out it does not leave room for 'rights'.

13.2 Criticisms of Utilitarianism

- A judge who applies a Utilitarianism approach would determine their decisions by attempting to determine what judge would be the best for the general good.

- Utilitarianism can be rule-oriented, but not overly simplistic about it.
  - For example, it might argue for treating certain people in a way that might not be good in the short term but would result in a long-term benefit for all.
- The primary criticism is that the theory focuses so much on the good of the whole that it ignores individuals.
  - The argument is usually that the theory ignores *individual* rights.
  - For example, even if one could see that the general good was enhanced by the killing of an individual (capital punishment), many would still feel that it was wrong.

13.3 Liberty and Equality as Liberal Concepts

- The concepts of 'liberty' and 'equality' have been in the forefront of societal, political, and legal developments for the last 500 years.
- Both of these concepts are rooted in 'morality' or moral thinking, though many would deny or ignore that observation.
- The famous lawyer, judge, and legal theorist, Patrick Devlin (1905–1992) wrote about these issues and morality when he wrote:
  - it is what the ordinary 'man on the Clapham omnibus' thinks,
  - in which he firmly believes,
  - and can be enforced with criminal sanctions (because he holds them so strongly).
- Hart, on the other hand, does not believe that what the ordinary person thinks is grounded in 'moral rightness'

  - He does not believe that just doing something 'wrong' is reason enough for a criminal sanction to be levied against someone.
  - Along John Stuart Mill, he believes that the only enforcements should come when someone does something that interferes with the freedoms of others.

13.4 Approaches to Morality

- Dworkin outlines the 'concept of a moral position
  - An ordinary person's reactions can be irrational, prejudiced, a gut-reaction, or mere parroting of what they have heard.
  - Dworkin says that none of these responses are a 'wrong' moral point of view.
- Jonathan Glover (1941–) follows a similar line of argument.
  - Moral arguments between people can be based on facts, or not based on facts
  - To resolve them, it is necessary to go back to 'ultimate axioms' — core assumptions and beliefs that ground our moral and ethics beliefs.
  - Yet these can be blurred or incoherent.
- Dworkin and Glover believe that moral arguments are not *just* subjective opinions, but are capable of being rational issues of thought and debate.
- Every argument or viewpoint could be a moral one (even if not valid).
  - If a person's views can be supported with some degree of rationality and facts, then it can be valid.

- On the other hand, a person can be mistaken, or have beliefs based on incorrect facts, or believe incorrectly, if their views do not reach that threshold of rationality.

13.5 Equality

- Some argue that equality should be seen in how we treat others, rather than on some scale of all being 'equal'.
- This way of viewing 'equality' focuses more on seeing people as individuals, with a certain point of view, and treating that 'fairly,' than in some political or legal system of laws that 'makes' people (plural) equal.

13.6 Economics of Law Approach

- The Chicago School of Law has analyzed the law terms of 'cost-effectiveness'.
- The method employed used the Kaldor-Hicks criterion (reallocation of resources that compensates those who are worse off by those who are better off and able to handle it)
  - This is a less stringent approach than the Pareto efficiency model (allocating resources until it is impossible to make one better off without making another worse off)
- This way of viewing judicial decisions is utilitarian, because it looks at the maximum efficiency of the system.
- One of the criticism of this model is that if legal rights are allocated (like economic resources), then the allocation must necessarily come before a judicial decision is rendered.

14. Feminist Legal Theory

14.1 Deconstruction and Reconstruction

- Gender divisions make up a lot of roles and divisions in almost all societies.
  - Feminist analysis and critique questions these divisions
  - Feminist jurisprudence analyzes and critiques how law and a legal system supports division and hierarchy regarding gender.
  - Feminist theories of patriarchy call into question the power expressed in these divisions among both private and public view society.
  - Feminist theories seek to change the more oppressive divisions for women in subcultural, cultural, and global areas.
- The 'Second Wave' of feminist legal theory attempted to deconstruct what was seen as male-dominated concepts of political and legal theories.
  - This approach was negative and deconstructive
  - It called into questions the universality of ideas of power, freedom, authority, privacy, democracy, citizenship
  - It sought to discover what post-patriarchal society could be and if it was even possible.
- Some of the approaches in the writings of these theorists:

- Claimed that injuries and harm to women are often dismissed as trivial, humorous, self-induced, biological, etc.
  - Seeks to find connections between private and local violence against women and violence in the name of a State or community.
- Critiquing the approach and assumptions of traditional jurisprudence and philosophical thought in the Western world.
  - Much of what is seen as objective and generalizing have actually not been so, because they proceed from a purely masculine point of view.
  - Any concept of dualism is suspect.

- Critiquing 'abstract masculinity' as it impacts how society is organized and what its suppositions are (often called 'Asking the Woman Question').
  - The rule of law can distort one's understanding of relationships relationships
  - Carol Gilligan (1936–) critiques Kohlberg's theory
    - which states that cannot reach higher stages of reasoning because they focus on the relational aspect of interpersonal relationships.
    - She argues that what it considered 'normal' has been organized by male thinking.
    - Laws intended to seek equality are really just trying to make women more like men.
    - See also the work of Catherine MacKinnon (1946–)
- Attempting to draw out and analyze voices that have traditionally been excluded from meta-narrative of modern society (of both women and also of ethnic minorities)
  - Attempts to focus on the real experience of these voices which are lost in traditional methods of logical writing.

  - Patricia J. Williams (1951–) has sought to do this by writing reflections about personal experience rather than standard legal theory and method.
  - This approach asks how traditional legal writing and theory states conclusions in absolutes without taking into account the complexity of these issues.
- A critique of many dualistic models for understanding society as it stands today: public/private, mothering/fathering, biology/culture, fixed gender identity, etc.).
  - Sees gender as one element among many others (class, race, ethnicity, age, sexual orientation, etc.).
  - Williams criticized those who prefer to ignore suffering and exploitation (a 'culture of complacency').
  - Attacked the concept of 'reification' (where social issues are only addressed when they are fitted into the categories and concepts of legal theory).

The French Revolution

- Many suggest that the French Revolution was a pivotal expression of modern liberal rights as it related to law.
- The event and its aftermath made the concepts of liberalism part of social reality.
  - For example, the creation of divorce laws in 1792, the reaction against them in the Napoleonic Civil Code (which were reversed after the restoration of the monarchy in 1815).
  - Marriage is seen as a civil contract.
- Changing of inheritance laws.

  The changes in divorce law led to changes in inheritance laws to make them equal for males and females.

- Avoidance of granting equal status of women in political affairs.
  - Women's role was the stability of the home.
  - Marquis de Sade went so far as to argue that women were sexual creatures and should be available for all men.
- Joan Scott (1941–) and Carol Pateman (1940–) argue that the goals of feminism will not be reached through the ideas of liberal political theory,
  - early concepts of feminist thought from the Revolution on were opposed to liberal political theory
- Lynn Hunt (1945–)
  - States that traditional political life was considered 'rational, public, and universal'.
  - But women were excluded because they were considered irrational, private, and particular-oriented.

14.2 History of Feminist Legal Theory

- Mary Wollstonecraft (1759 – 1797)
  - Wrote around the time of the French Revolution
  - Argued that although women could reason, traditional upbringing and roles suppressed the ability.
  - However, this could be remedied by changing the socialization patterns for children.
- The 'Suffragettes' of the 20th Century.
  - The focus and goal was primarily intended to secure the right to vote for women (and other rights).
  - Often called the 'first wave' of feminism.
- The modern women's liberation movement (the 1960s and later)

- Often called the 'second wave' of feminism
- Came out of the larger movements for civil rights.
- Sought freedom and equality for women
  - work outside of the home
  - reproductive rights
  - freedom over their own bodies and sexuality.

- Nicola Lacey
  - Argues that the first wave grew out of a liberalist concern and sought the same status and protection that males possessed
    - Lacey critiques it because it used the male standard as the solution.
  - The second wave focused more on women's experience and argued for 'different but equal'.
  - This approach had the drawback of inviting the old arguments about the natural subordination of women.
- The third wave is more reflective because it asked 'the woman question'
  - Seeks to understand gender roles and how they operate in the legal and social structures.

14.3 Feminist Views and Universalism

-Feminist criticism helps to analyze issues of human agency and the human condition

- It emphasizes how people deal with circumstances and prob-lcms,
  - Feminist legal critique uses this approach to examine possible actions and identities in the larger legal and social order

  – It also examines how those activities result in social identity.

– An important methodology is to attempt deconstruction of the perceive 'male' common sense, and to create a new way of discussing social and legal issues.

  – This requires addresses the conflicts between

    – the particular and the universal

    – the concrete and the abstract.

– Concepts of Universalism are present in the suffragette and liberal feminist movements.

– Other movements, cultural feminism, seek a unique and particular subject-formations for women.

– Others attempt to integrate multiple subject-formations (class, race, ethnicity, and sexual orientation).

The Liberal Approach

– Stresses the rule of law.

– The second wave of feminism attempted to reveal inequality between the sexes.

– This method argued that women should be treated the same as men.

– Criticized by some because it still used male-oriented patterns and structures, so women had to become like men.

The 'Ethics of Care' Approach

– Differences between the genders are something to be celebrated.

– Gilligan noted that two distinct moral codes corresponded to gender.

  - The feminine moral code is based on caring, maintenance of relationships, communication, and concern for the particular needs of others in their own context. (The Ethics of Care).
  - The masculine moral code is objective, impartial, impersonal, emotional, obligation-oriented, and focused on justice, rights, and rules. The ethic of justice. (The Ethics of Justice).
  - This was in opposition to Lawrence Kohlberg's work, which identified five stages of moral development.
- Seyla Benhabib has discussed the consequences of the feminine code:
  - Both moral codes need to be considered together and need to interact and inform one another
  - There should not be a clear line between them for private and public life.
- Some have critiques Gilligan's work because it is based on a small sample.
  - What about global differences?
  - Different socialization?
  - Different biologies?
- Robin West
  - Argues that women crave intimacy and connection with other people, as opposed to a separate autonomy (a liberal legal value).
  - Therefore, liberal legal jurisprudence works against women
  - What is needed is a feminist jurisprudence approach.

Radical Feminist Approaches

- Catherine McKinnon (1946–)

  - The differences between men and women are structured hierarchically in society
  - They have been structured by men to benefit men.
  - She compares this gender structure as a Marxist power structure.
  - She criticizes both the 'sameness' approach and 'difference' approach because both are still based on structures set up by men. d
- Criticisms of her approach are that the theory is flawed because it assumes women are passive victims.
- Others view this approach (and the ethic of care approach) as attempting to construct universal standard for all women
  - Which is as much a problem as trying to use a standard set up by males
  - Replaces the male standard with a single female standard.

Ethnic Minority Feminists

- Began as a criticism that theorists were emphasizing gender classification over other social classifications (race, class, geographically, culture).
  - The feminist theories neglected to analyze how these social classifications interacted and affected gender issues.
  - Mariana Valverde, for example, has noted the juxtaposition of a woman who pick coffee beans for $.50 a day in Brazil with the white American feminist who sips that coffee as she writes about women 'in general.'
- Other perspectives focus on issues of domestic women in the context of a modern family while ignoring the racial and ethnic dimensions of domestic helpers (nannies, housemaids).

- Postmodernists and cultural relativists argue that seeking some universal truth of justice for women will fail because of these issues.
  - It would be an approach with its structures of thought based in neocolonial and new imperialistic considerations.
- Post-modern feminists reject the idea of this 'false consciousness' with its fixed identities based on a universal view of a gender.
- Other criticize this approach as weakening the feminist movements
  - Because such movements must have some standard of identity to measure inequality against
  - This critique would be true of any radical legal theory, because if one every perspective is valid, then how does one determine which is 'better' and 'worse'?

14.4 The Future

- Recent works have argued that the way forward is a return to classic progressive political programs
  - because feminism was rooted in pointing out injustices
- Human rights law as based on the concept that all individuals deserve to be treated the same without regard to their gender, racial, ethnic, religious, or any other identity.
  - Some argue that feminism, then, is merely one part of discussing human rights.
  - The old liberal theory which focused on rights, freedom, any quality is still valid being revisited by many feminists
- These theorist are not arguing that nothing needs to change, but that this is a better ground to start.

COURSE DIAGRAMS

Introduction

These diagrams offer a visual aid to all the topics and subtopics in the same order as the Course Outlines, including the key terms, cases, and statutes.

Suggested study plan:

1. Look over the chapter which corresponds to the chapter you are studying.
2. Read your assigned readings and do any assigned activities.
3. Review the Course Outline for the current subject, then the VisuaLaw Diagrams. See if you can discuss each item in detail just by looking at the Diagrams. Go back over the reading material to strengthen the areas in which you are weak.
4. Come back and repeat this periodically for each chapter throughout the course.

When you are preparing for your exams, use the VisuaLaw Diagrams as an aid to memorization and to test yourself on the topics. Test yourself by recreating the diagrams from memory until. Pretend you are teaching the topic to someone else.

3. Hobbes, Bentham, and Austin

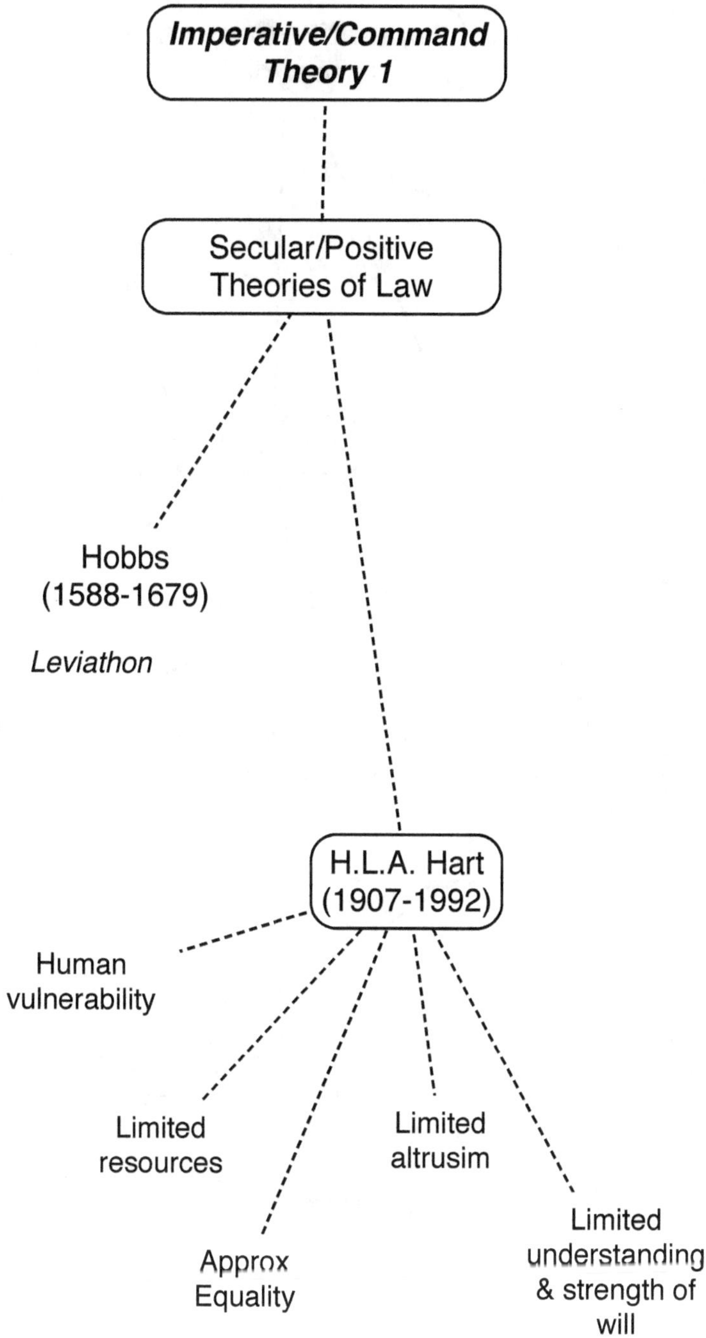

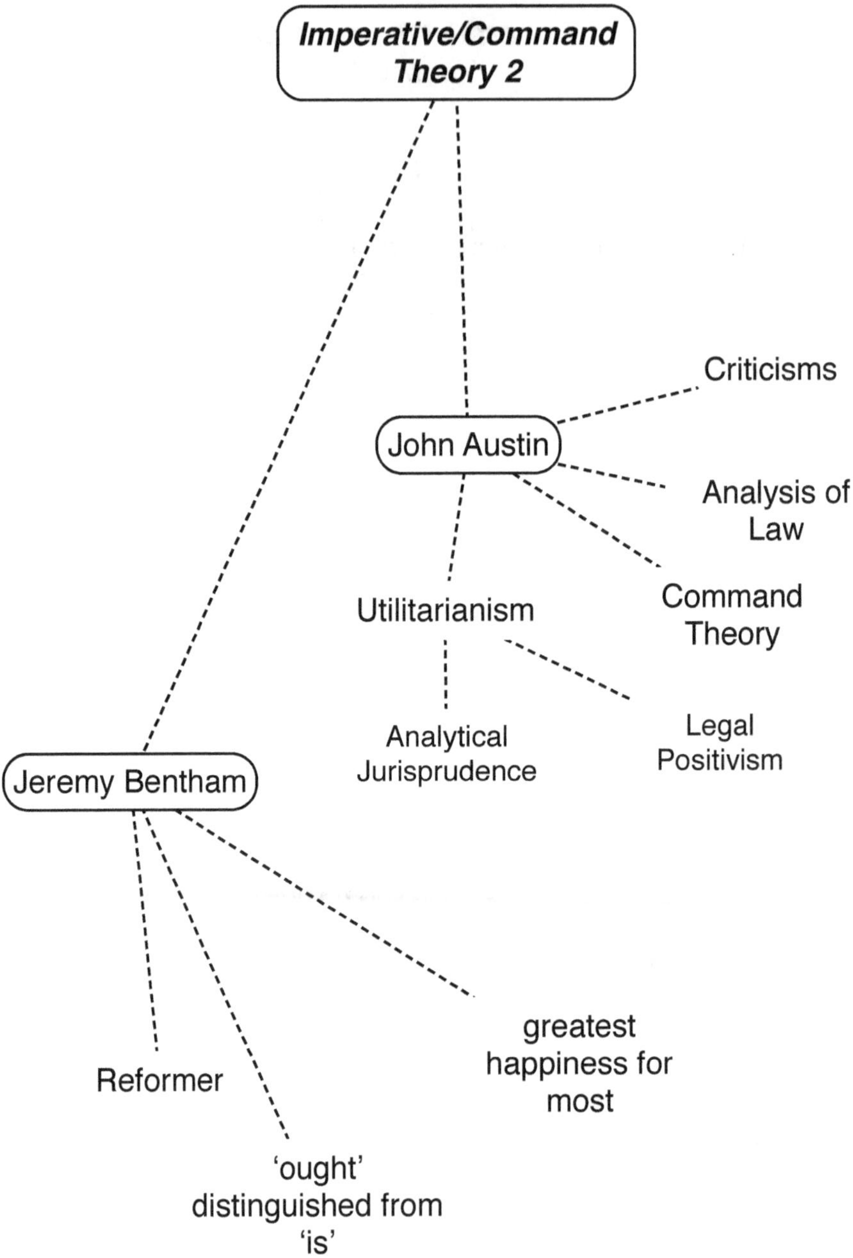
Imperative/Command Theory 2
John Austin
Criticisms
Analysis of Law
Command Theory
Utilitarianism
Analytical Jurisprudence
Legal Positivism
Jeremy Bentham
Reformer
'ought' distinguished from 'is'
greatest happiness for most

4. Natural Law Theory

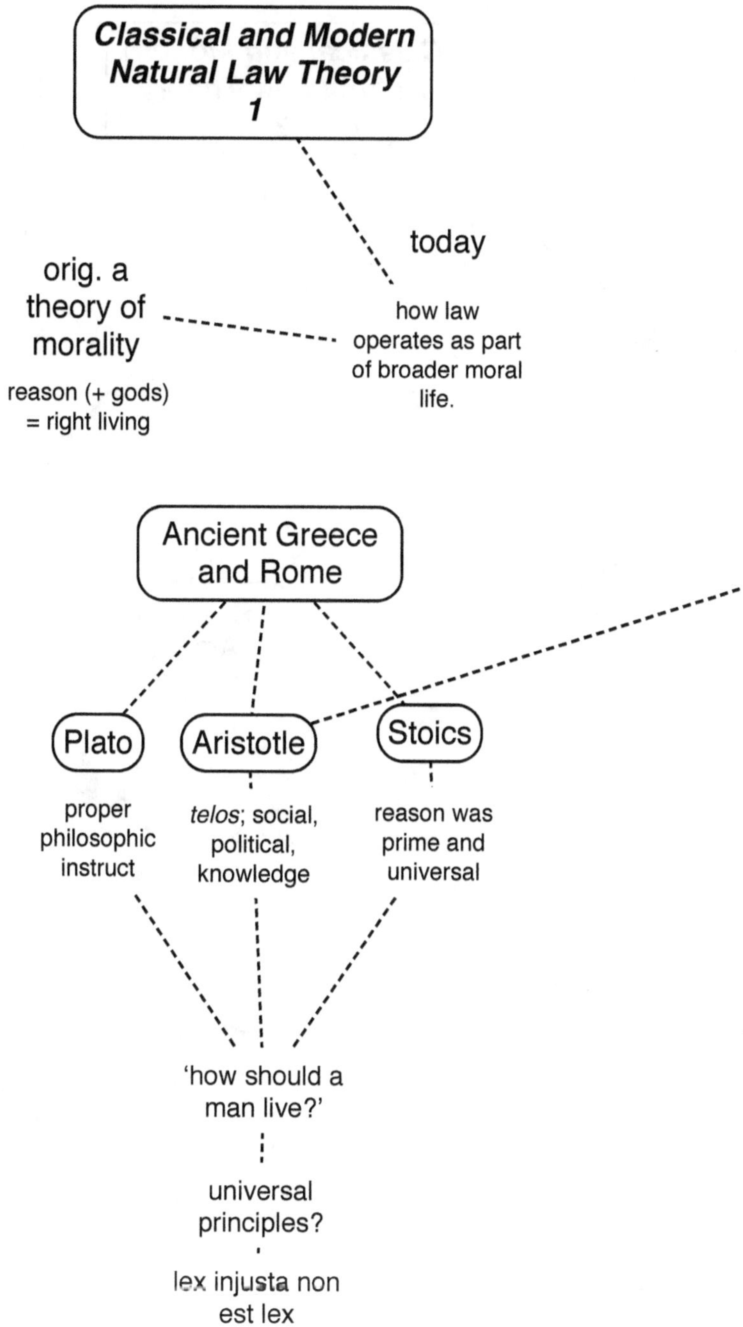

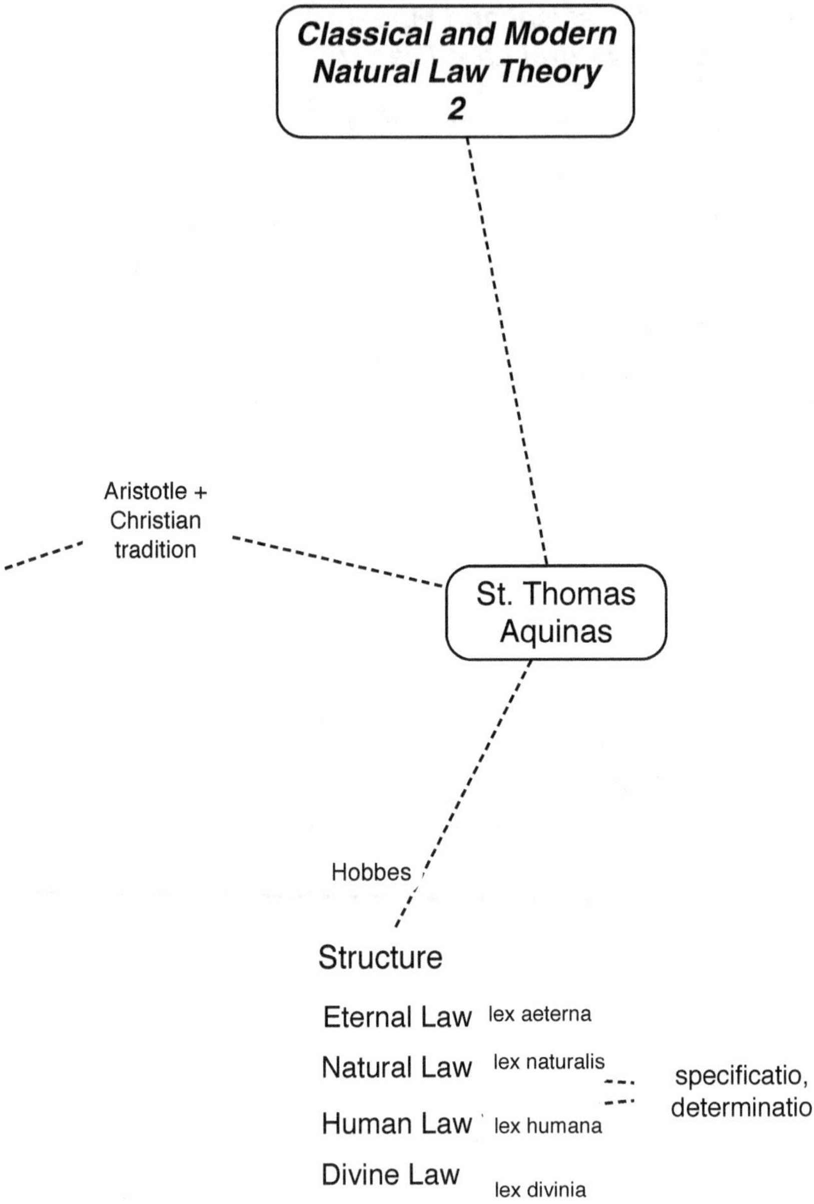
Classical and Modern Natural Law Theory 2
St. Thomas Aquinas
Aristotle + Christian tradition
Hobbes
Structure
Eternal Law lex aeterna
Natural Law lex naturalis
Human Law lex humana
Divine Law lex divinia
specificatio, determinatio

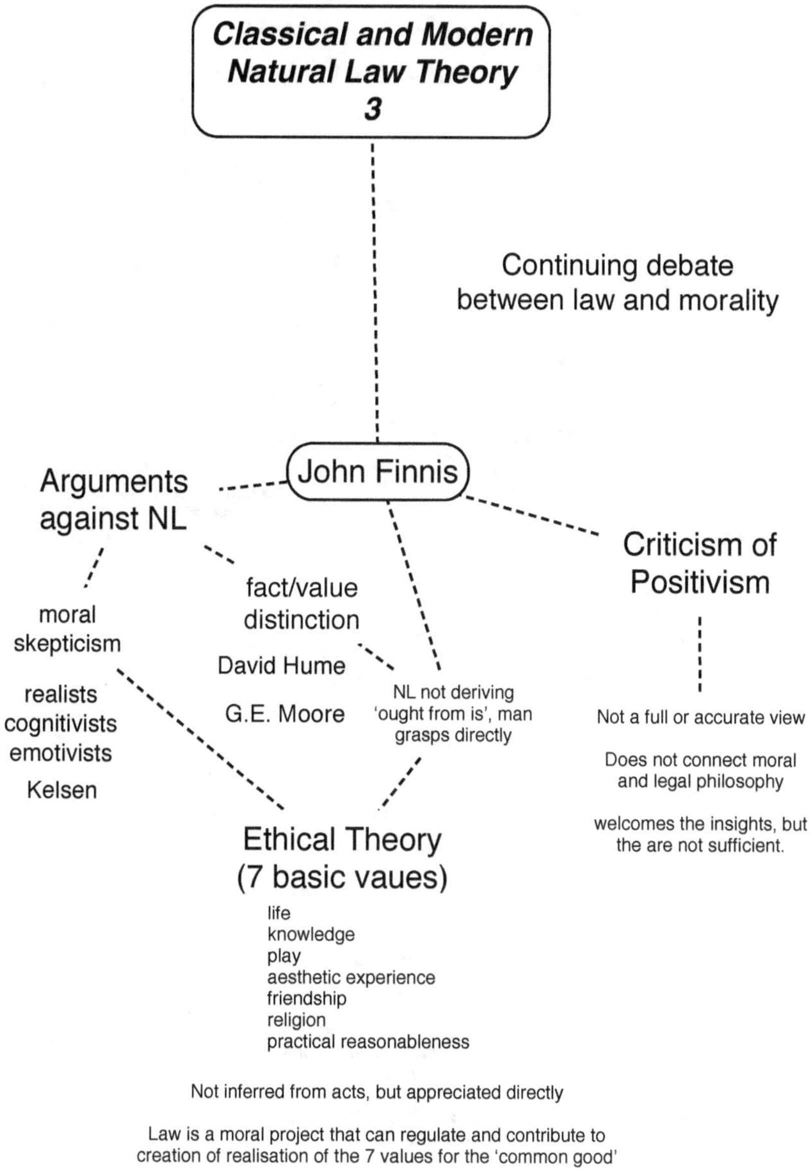
Classical and Modern
Natural Law Theory
3
Continuing debate
between law and morality
John Finnis
Arguments
against NL
moral
skepticism
realists
cognitivists
emotivists
Kelsen
fact/value
distinction
David Hume
G.E. Moore
NL not deriving
'ought from is', man
grasps directly
Criticism of
Positivism
Not a full or accurate view
Does not connect moral
and legal philosophy
welcomes the insights, but
the are not sufficient.
Ethical Theory
(7 basic vaues)
life
knowledge
play
aesthetic experience
friendship
religion
practical reasonableness
Not inferred from acts, but appreciated directly
Law is a moral project that can regulate and contribute to
creation of realisation of the 7 values for the 'common good'

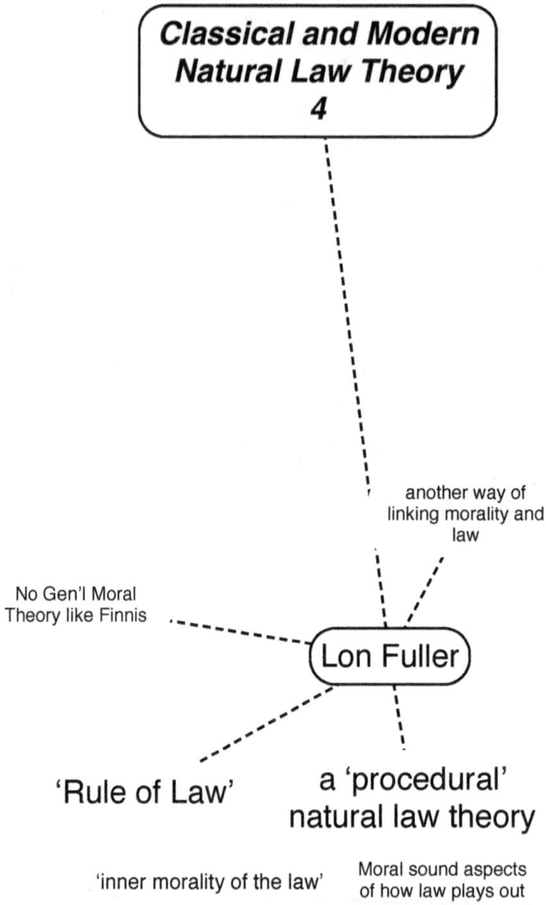

8 desiderata

operate by gen'l rules
published
prospectively not retrospectively
reasonably clear and intelligible
not contradictory
not change too often or radically
do not require the impossib;e
administered with meaning and purpose

5. HLA Hart's: The Concept of Law

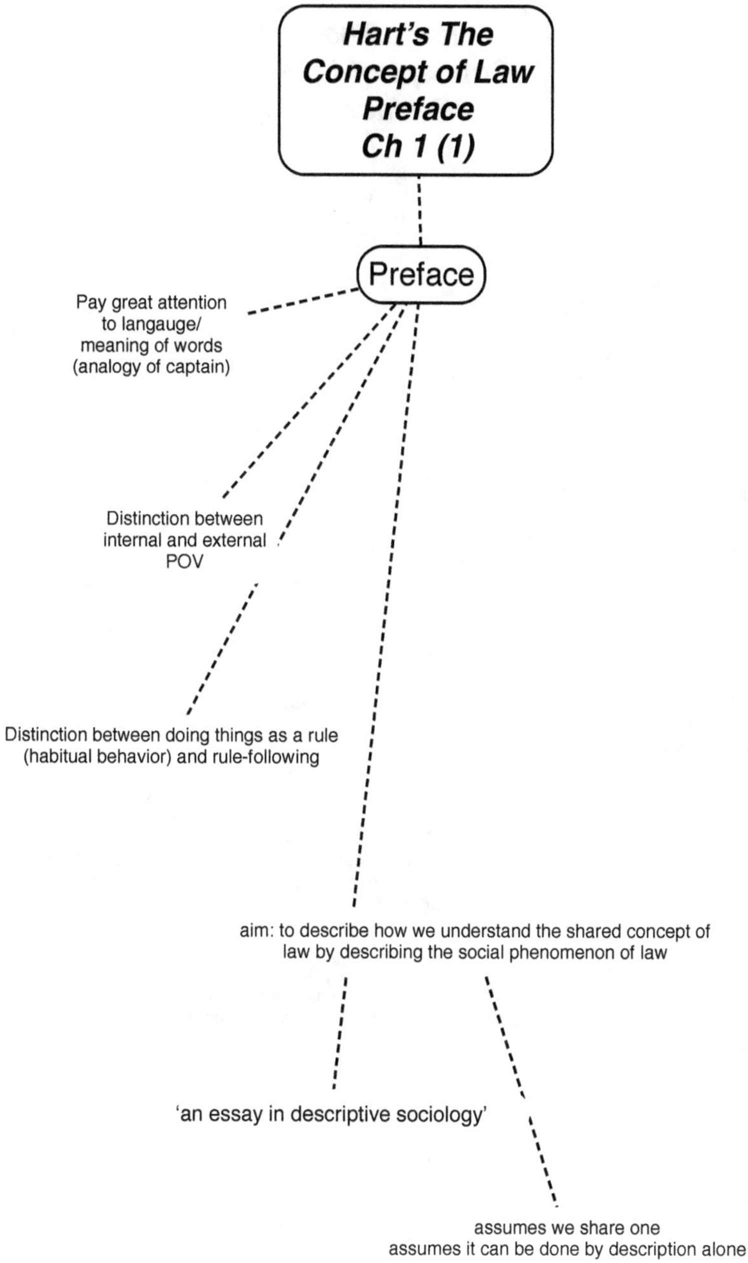

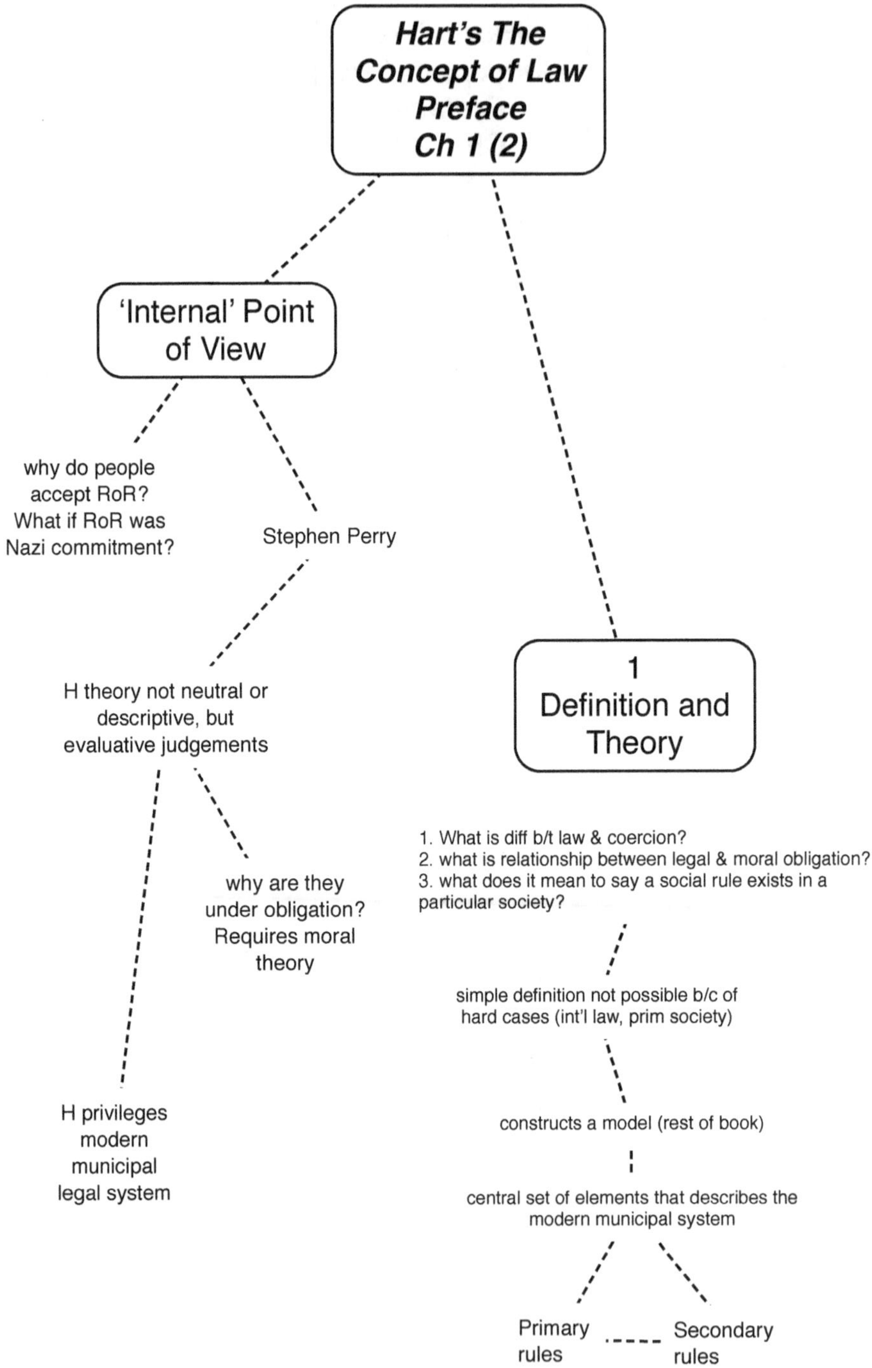
Hart's The Concept of Law Preface Ch 1 (2)
'Internal' Point of View
why do people accept RoR? What if RoR was Nazi commitment?
Stephen Perry
H theory not neutral or descriptive, but evaluative judgements
why are they under obligation? Requires moral theory
H privileges modern municipal legal system
1 Definition and Theory
1. What is diff b/t law & coercion?
2. what is relationship between legal & moral obligation?
3. what does it mean to say a social rule exists in a particular society?
simple definition not possible b/c of hard cases (int'l law, prim society)
constructs a model (rest of book)
central set of elements that describes the modern municipal system
Primary rules
Secondary rules

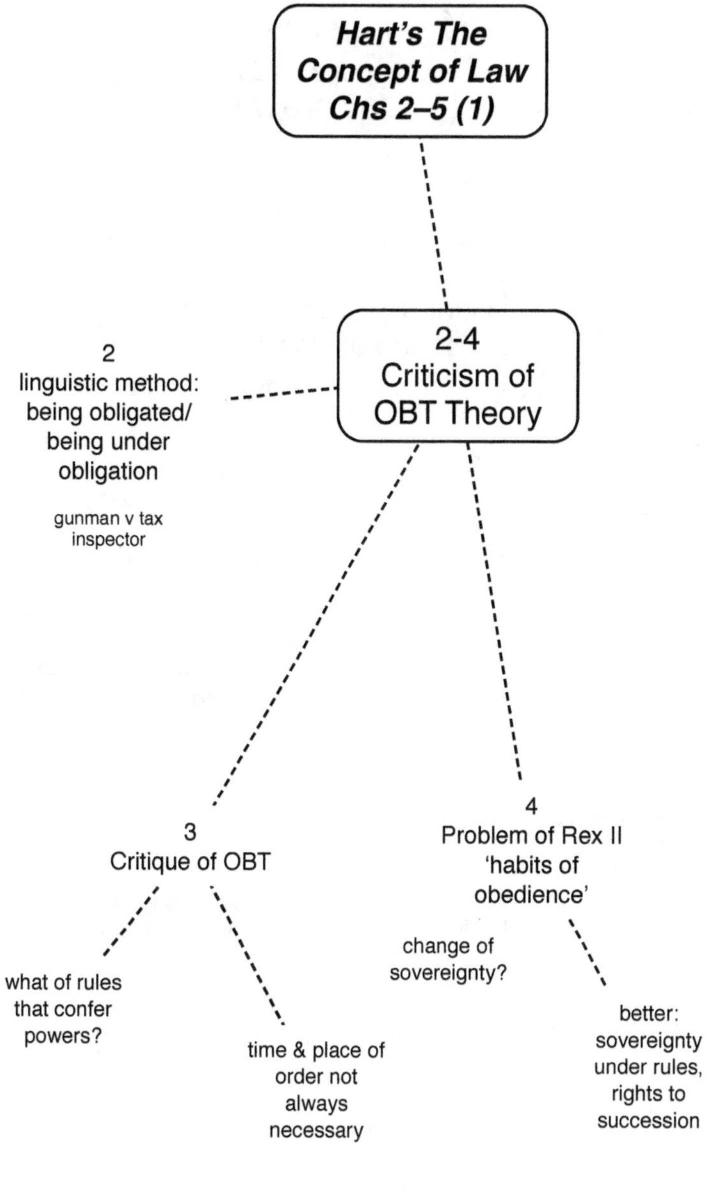
Hart's The Concept of Law Chs 2–5 (1)
2-4 Criticism of OBT Theory
2
linguistic method: being obligated/ being under obligation
gunman v tax inspector
3
Critique of OBT
what of rules that confer powers?
time & place of order not always necessary
4
Problem of Rex II 'habits of obedience'
change of sovereignty?
better: sovereignty under rules, rights to succession

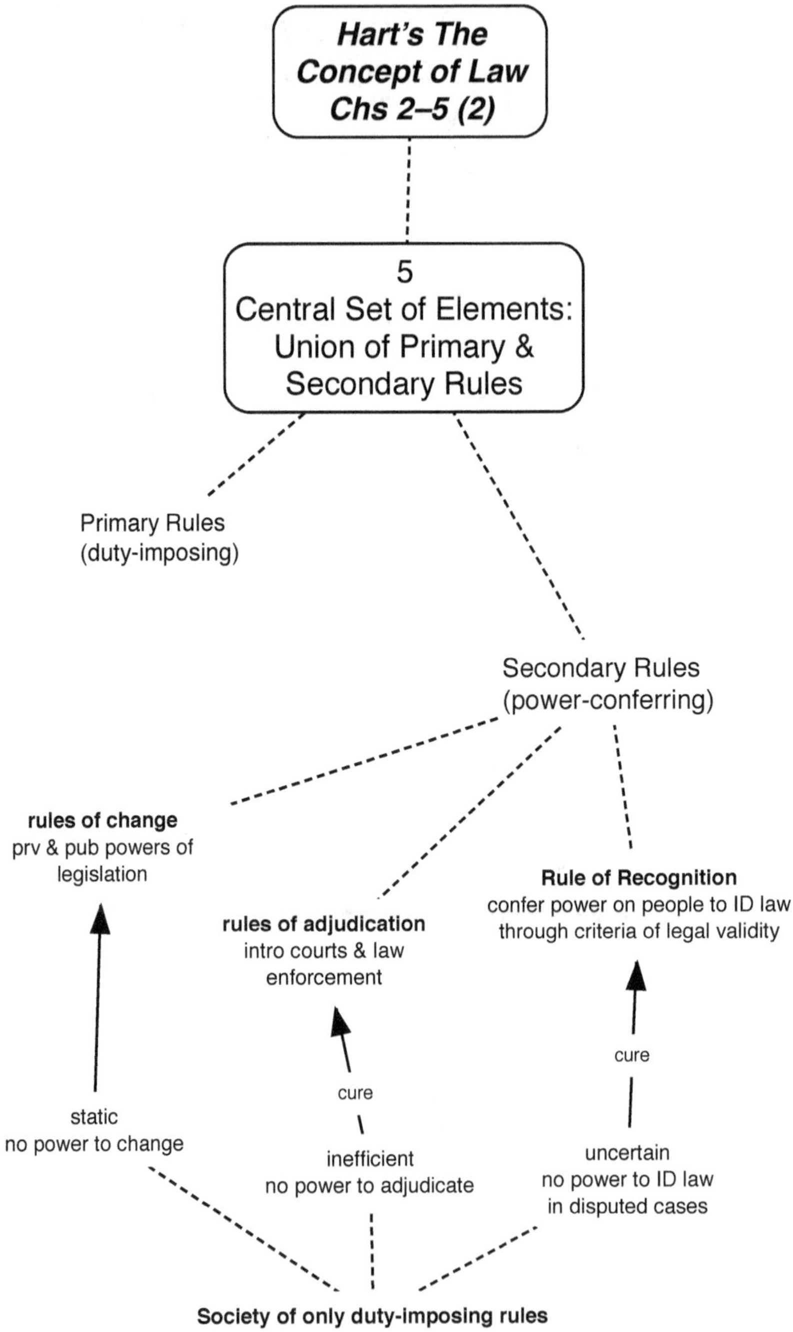
Hart's The Concept of Law Chs 2–5 (2)
5
Central Set of Elements: Union of Primary & Secondary Rules
Primary Rules (duty-imposing)
Secondary Rules (power-conferring)
rules of change
prv & pub powers of legislation
rules of adjudication
intro courts & law enforcement
Rule of Recognition
confer power on people to ID law through criteria of legal validity
cure
cure
static
no power to change
inefficient
no power to adjudicate
uncertain
no power to ID law in disputed cases
Society of only duty-imposing rules

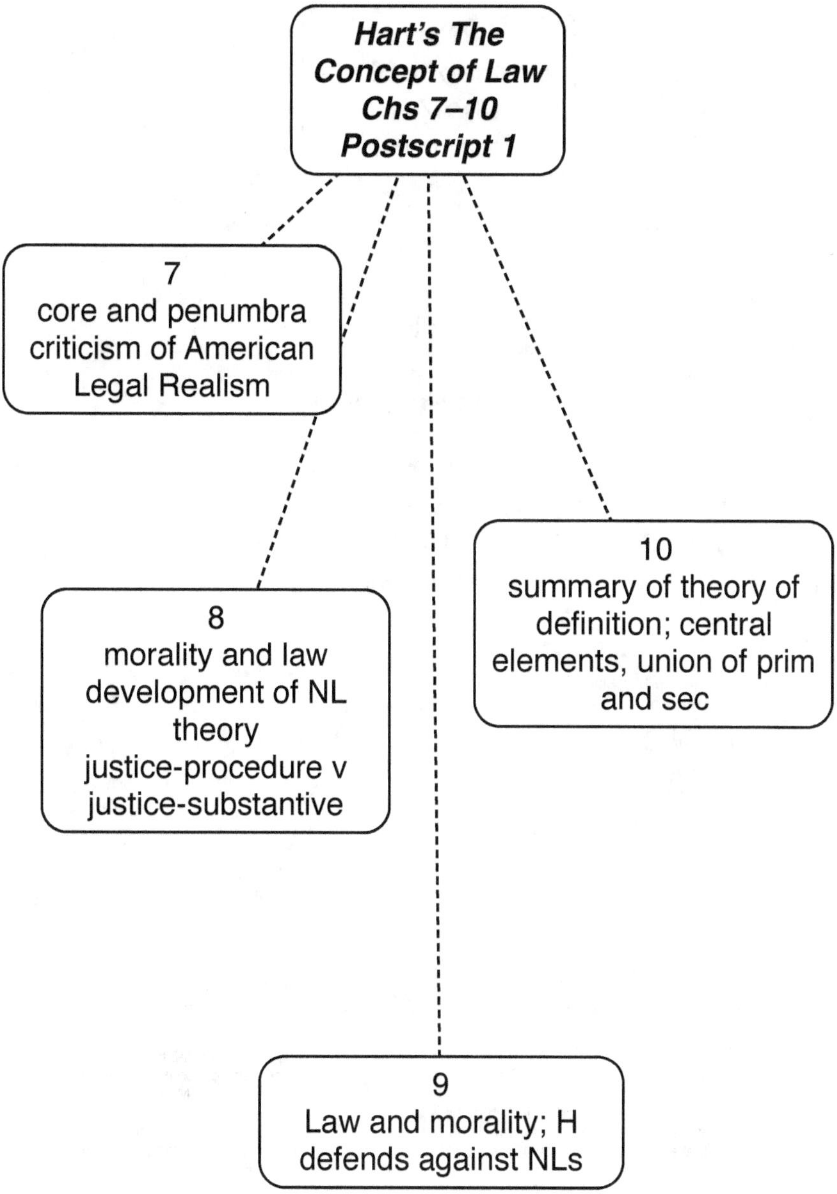
Hart's The Concept of Law Chs 7–10 Postscript 1
7
core and penumbra
criticism of American Legal Realism
8
morality and law
development of NL theory
justice-procedure v justice-substantive
9
Law and morality; H defends against NLs
10
summary of theory of definition; central elements, union of prim and sec

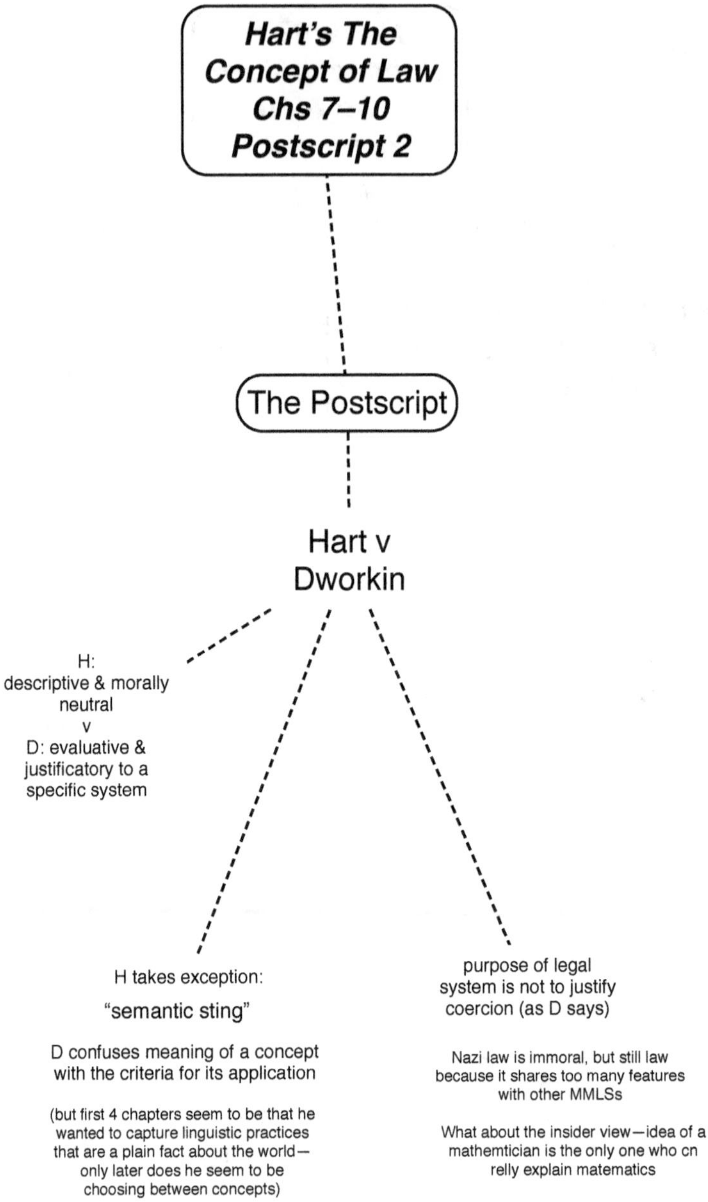
Hart's The Concept of Law Chs 7–10 Postscript 2
The Postscript
Hart v Dworkin
H: descriptive & morally neutral v D: evaluative & justificatory to a specific system
H takes exception:
"semantic sting"
D confuses meaning of a concept with the criteria for its application
(but first 4 chapters seem to be that he wanted to capture linguistic practices that are a plain fact about the world—only later does he seem to be choosing between concepts)
purpose of legal system is not to justify coercion (as D says)
Nazi law is immoral, but still law because it shares too many features with other MMLSs
What about the insider view—idea of a mathemtician is the only one who cn relly explain matematics

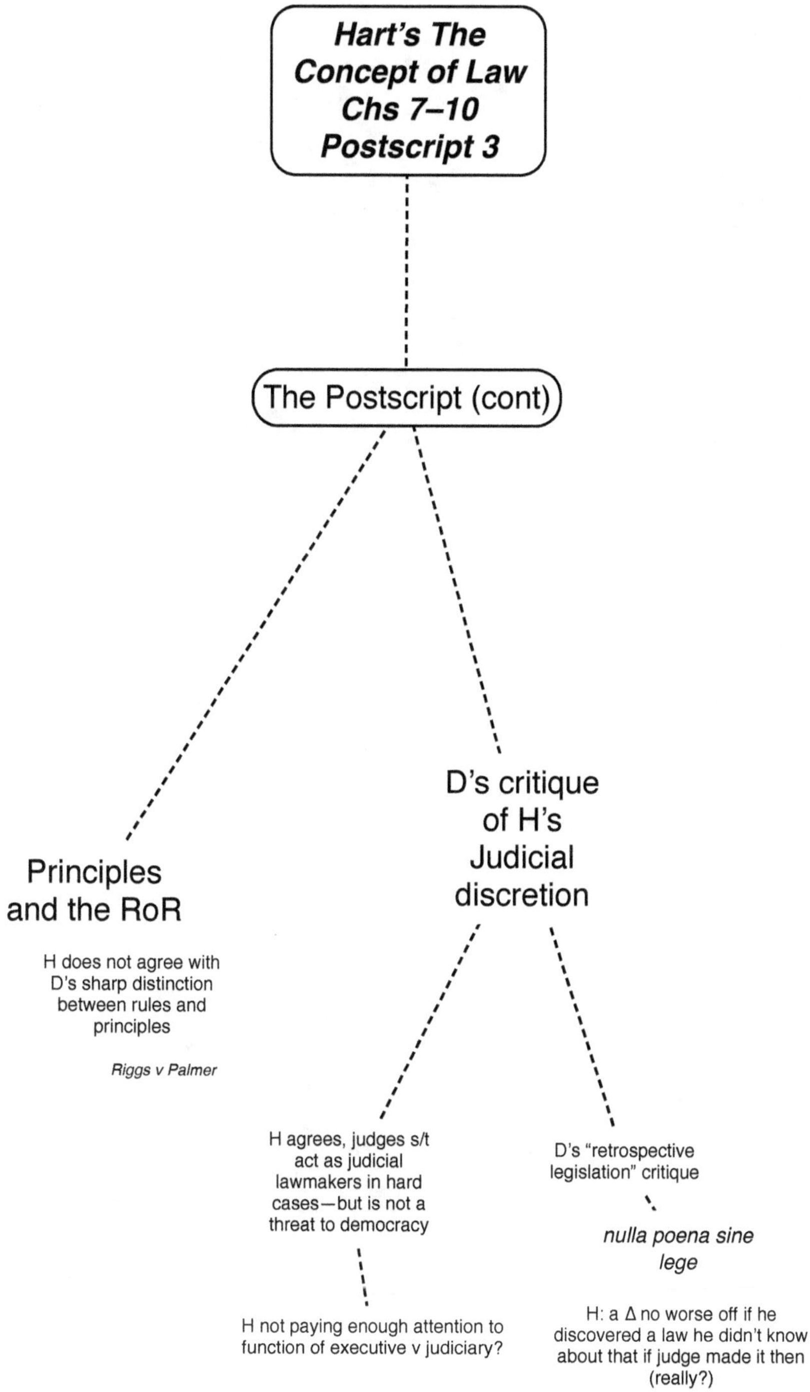
Hart's The Concept of Law Chs 7–10 Postscript 3
The Postscript (cont)
Principles and the RoR
H does not agree with D's sharp distinction between rules and principles
Riggs v Palmer
D's critique of H's Judicial discretion
H agrees, judges s/t act as judicial lawmakers in hard cases—but is not a threat to democracy
H not paying enough attention to function of executive v judiciary?
D's "retrospective legislation" critique
nulla poena sine lege
H: a Δ no worse off if he discovered a law he didn't know about that if judge made it then (really?)

6. Hart's Rule of Recognition

Hart's "Rule of Recognition" Ch 6 (1)

Critique

Finnis's critique

Natural Law and Natural Rights

RoR insufficiently explains WHAT sort of attitude officials have

(Finnis says moral acceptance)

(McCormick)

Dworkin's critique

Taking Rights Seriously, Ch 2

RoR is to 'cure defect of uncertainty:
any rule that cannot be ID'd with certainty must not be a law

but in hard cases:
- judges act as legislators
- apply retrospective law
- continually misdescribe what they do

(somust be something wrong with H's theory)

Example: s.51 Adoption Act 1951
R v Registrar of Births

No descriptive sense of what a rule is apart from interpretation (vehicles prohibited in the park)

(See H's core and penumbra, though)

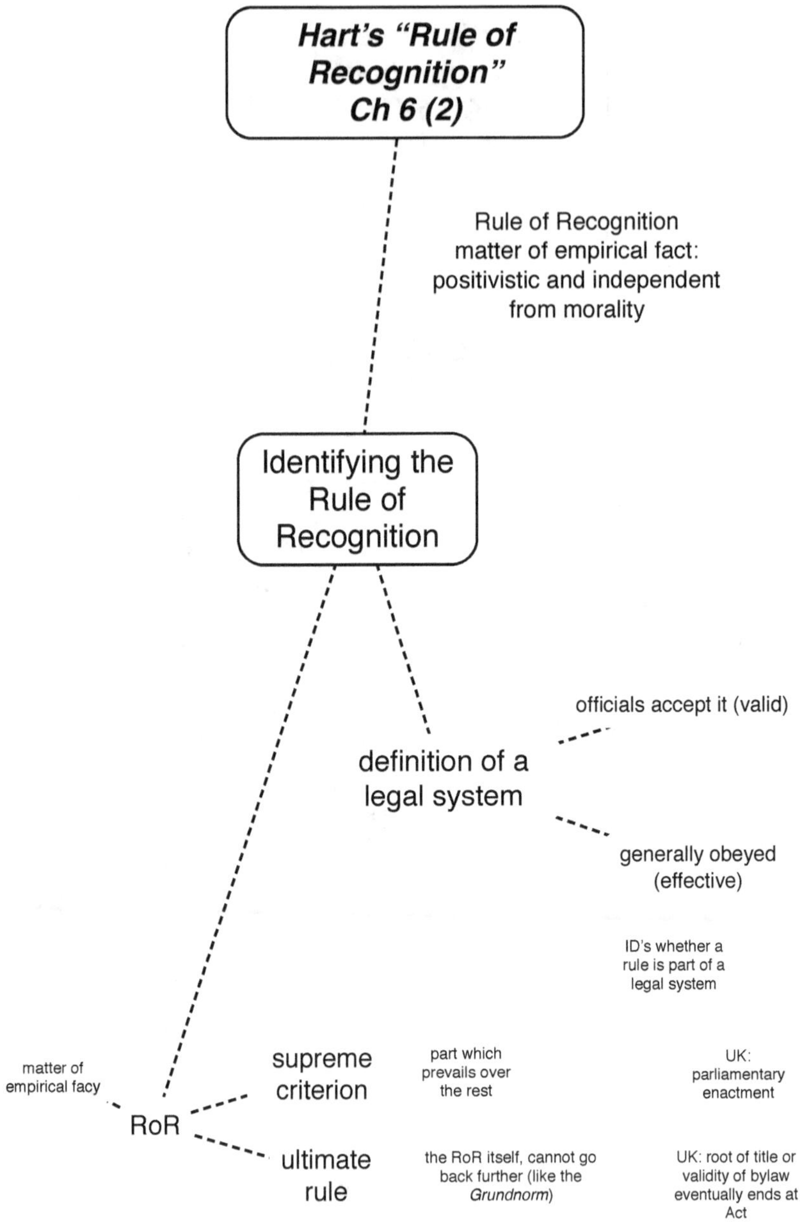
Hart's "Rule of Recognition" Ch 6 (2)
Rule of Recognition matter of empirical fact: positivistic and independent from morality
Identifying the Rule of Recognition
definition of a legal system
officials accept it (valid)
generally obeyed (effective)
ID's whether a rule is part of a legal system
matter of empirical facy
RoR
supreme criterion
part which prevails over the rest
UK: parliamentary enactment
ultimate rule
the RoR itself, cannot go back further (like the *Grundnorm*)
UK: root of title or validity of bylaw eventually ends at Act

7. Hart's Defenses Against Natural Law Theory & Fuller

Hart's Defense against natural law and Fuller's Criticism 1

Morality in the Penumbra of the Law

American Legal Realism → Hart's critiques

American Legal Realism

accused positivists of being formalistic and ignoring facts of adjudication & judicial lawmaking

real law occurs in courts; a rigid distinction between law & morality as positivism ignores what judges do

hard cases have an intersection of law and morality

Hart's critiques

There is a core settled meaning, as well as a penumbra of debatable cases

But it is still possible to make rational choices in the penumbra cases

Judges then are NOT debating what the law ought to be, then deicing what the law should be for the future, but are discovering what the law is by drawing out the latent meaning of the law.

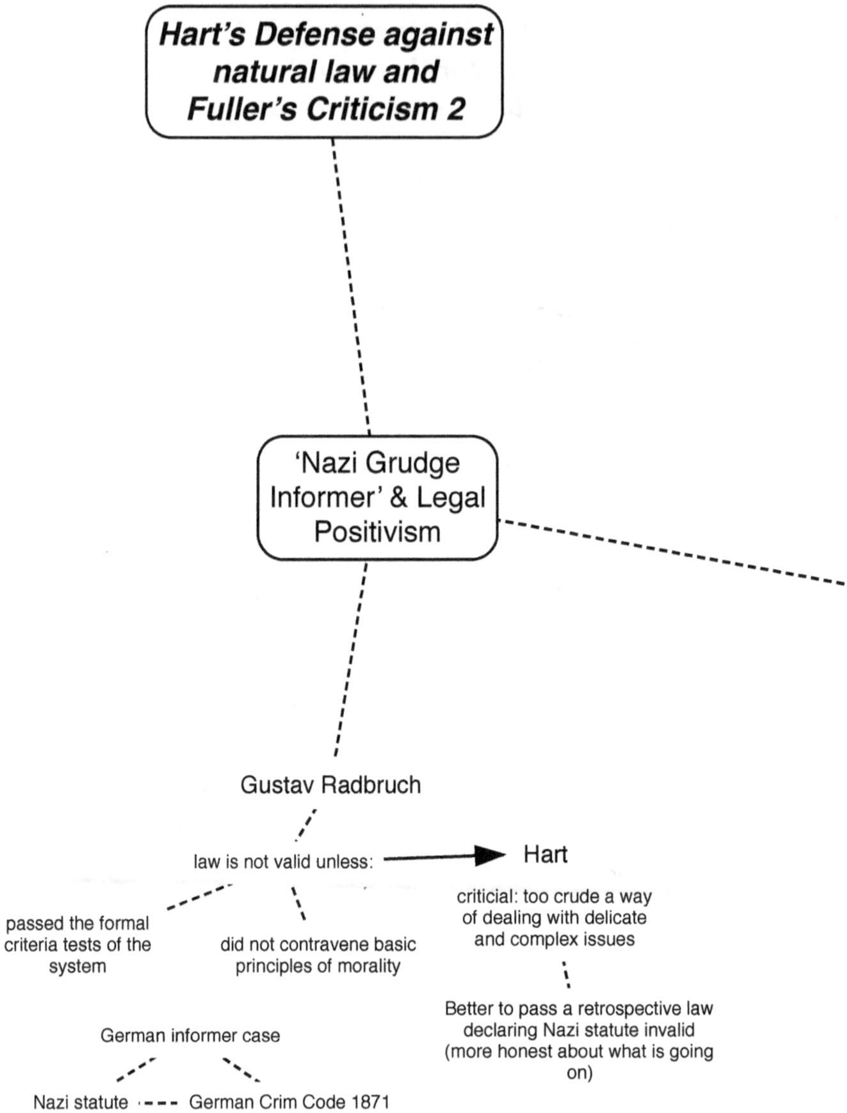
Hart's Defense against natural law and Fuller's Criticism 2
'Nazi Grudge Informer' & Legal Positivism
Gustav Radbruch
law is not valid unless:
Hart
passed the formal criteria tests of the system
did not contravene basic principles of morality
criticial: too crude a way of dealing with delicate and complex issues
Better to pass a retrospective law declaring Nazi statute invalid (more honest about what is going on)
German informer case
Nazi statute
German Crim Code 1871

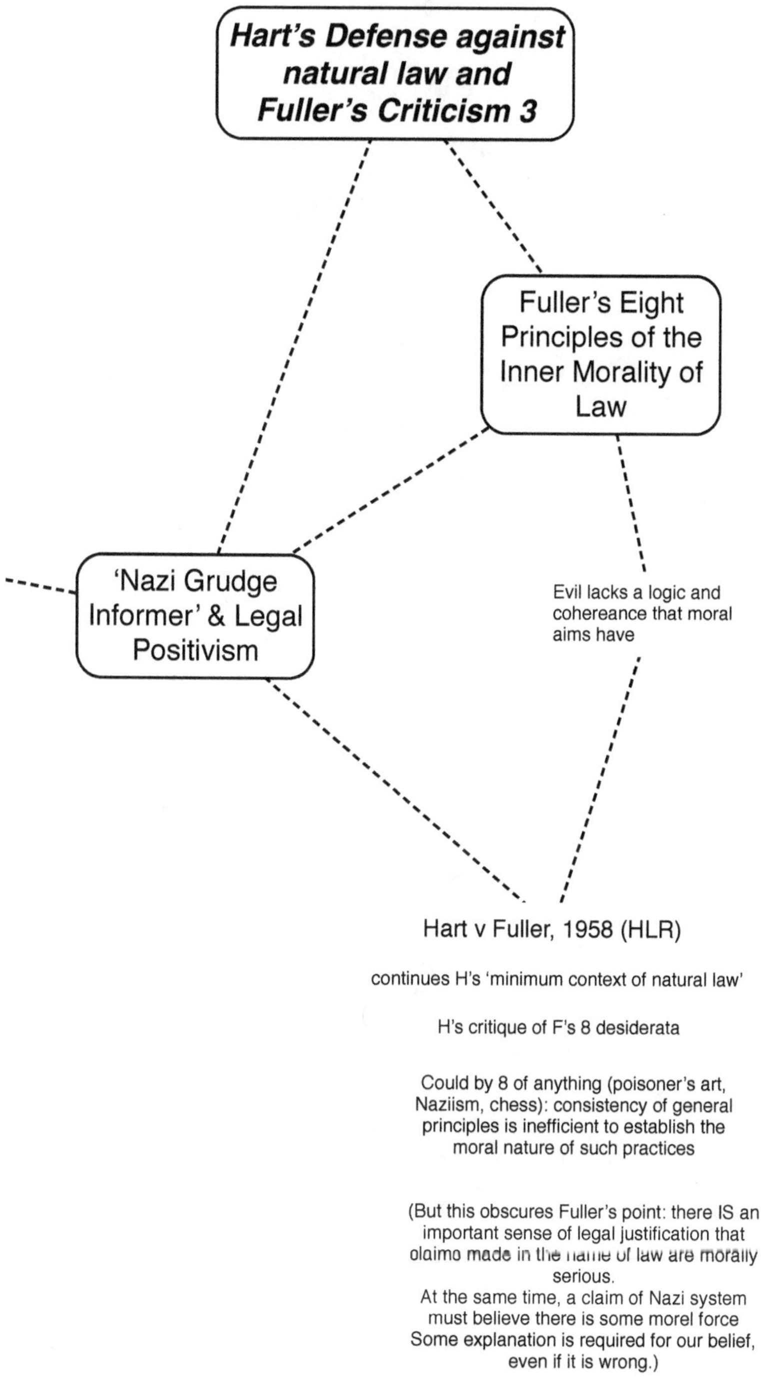
Hart's Defense against natural law and Fuller's Criticism 3
Fuller's Eight Principles of the Inner Morality of Law
'Nazi Grudge Informer' & Legal Positivism
Evil lacks a logic and cohereance that moral aims have
Hart v Fuller, 1958 (HLR)
continues H's 'minimum context of natural law'
H's critique of F's 8 desiderata
Could by 8 of anything (poisoner's art, Naziism, chess): consistency of general principles is inefficient to establish the moral nature of such practices
(But this obscures Fuller's point: there IS an important sense of legal justification that claims made in the name of law are morally serious.
At the same time, a claim of Nazi system must believe there is some morel force
Some explanation is required for our belief, even if it is wrong.)

8. Raz's Theory of Law: Service Conception

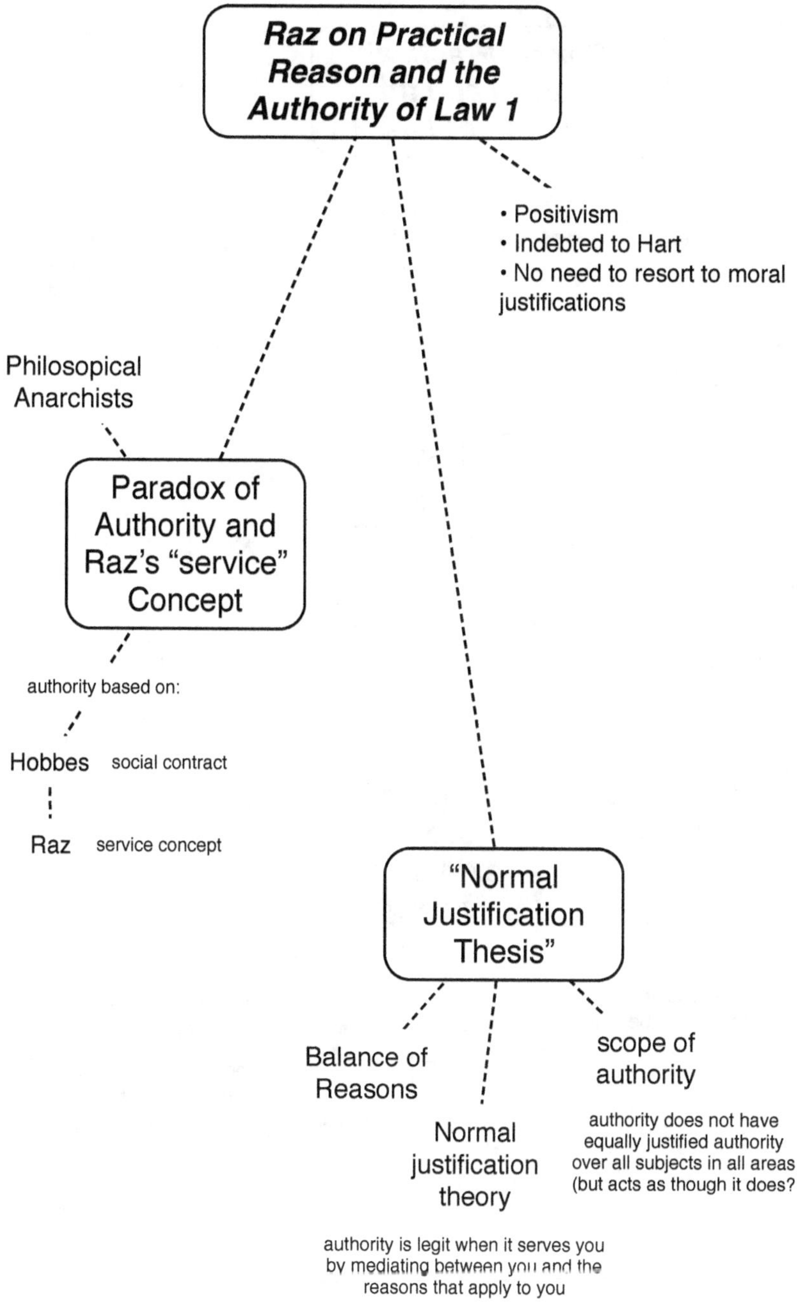

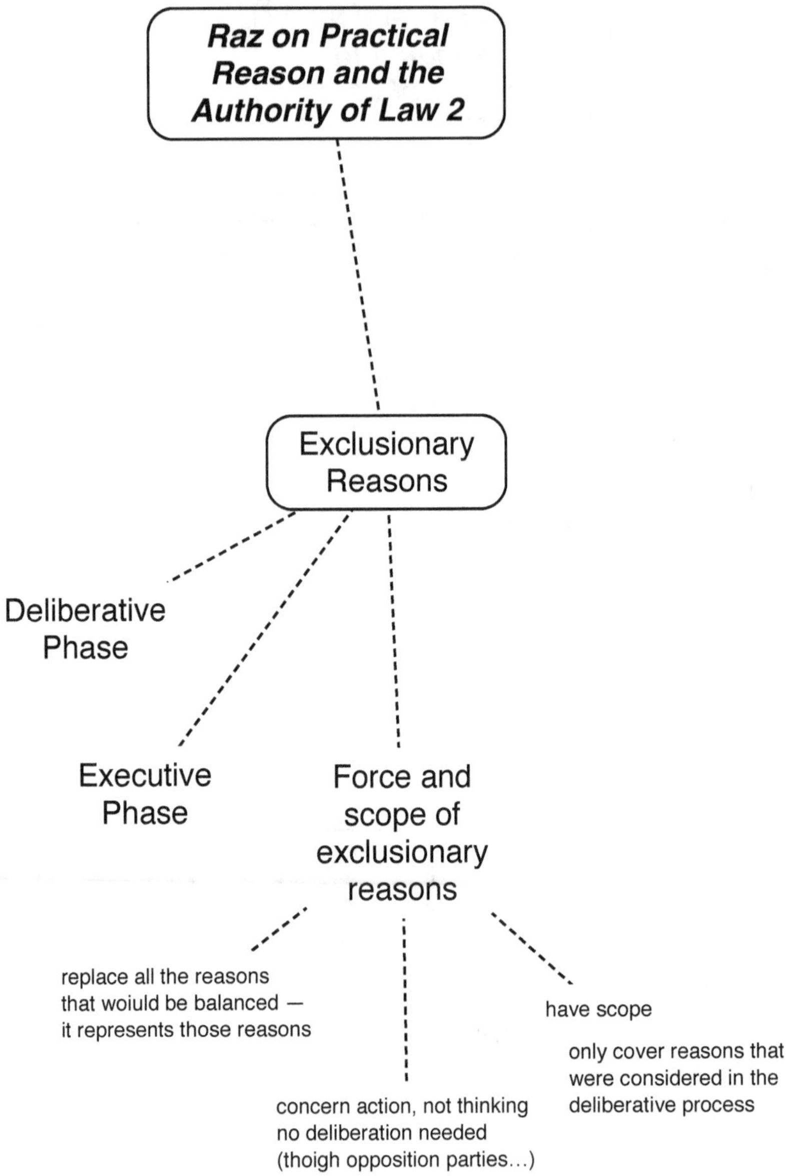
Raz on Practical Reason and the Authority of Law 2
Exclusionary Reasons
Deliberative Phase
Executive Phase
Force and scope of exclusionary reasons
replace all the reasons that woiuld be balanced — it represents those reasons
concern action, not thinking no deliberation needed (thoigh opposition parties…)
have scope
only cover reasons that were considered in the deliberative process

Raz on Practical Reason and the Authority of Law 3

Debate with Soft Positivists and Dworkin

SP: law incorporates what is moral
D: stronger than this; moral principles are not as resist to practical reason as R suggests
Raz: b/c morality is controversial it cannot be authoritative as law

Authority and Limits of the Law

practical v theoretical authoriy

Law claims authority

Limits of the law

- capable of mediating reasons/subjects
- by deliberating and directive
- must take the work away from subjects
- more or less specific
- (yet there are directives that are not ('act reasonably')
- not authoritative if it needs further deliberation

moral directives merely make a person weigh the balances

9. Practical Reason and the Law

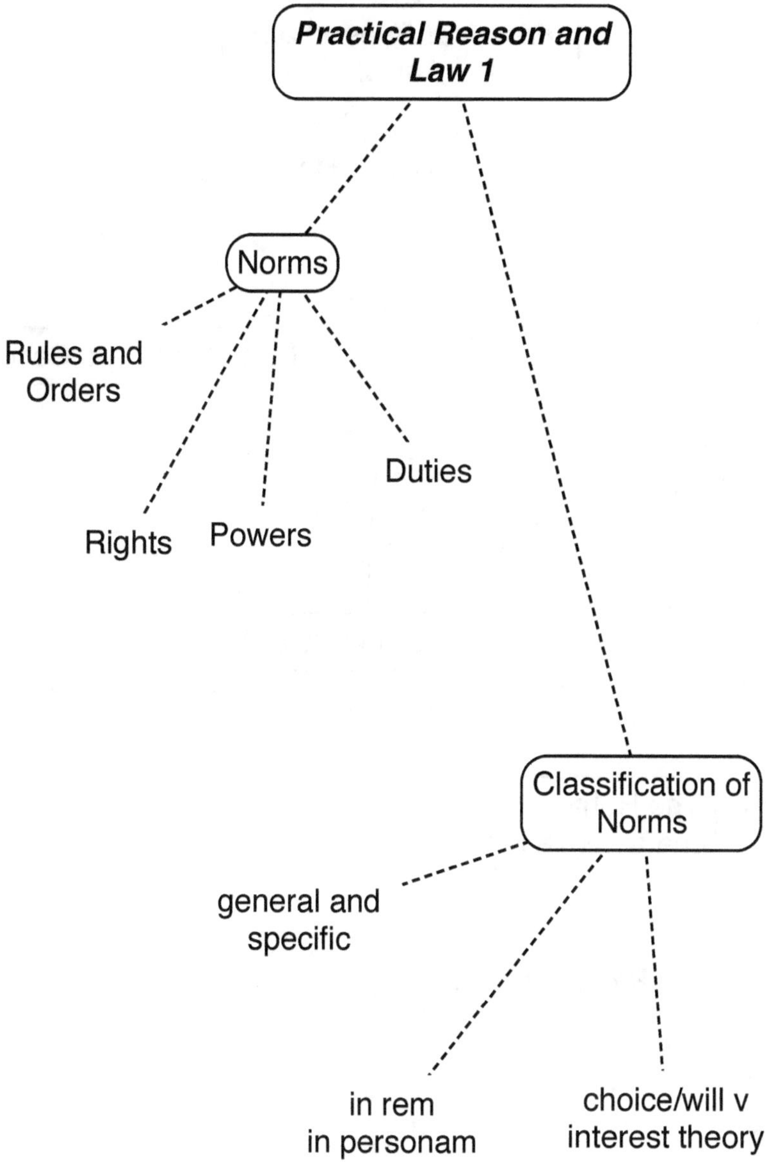

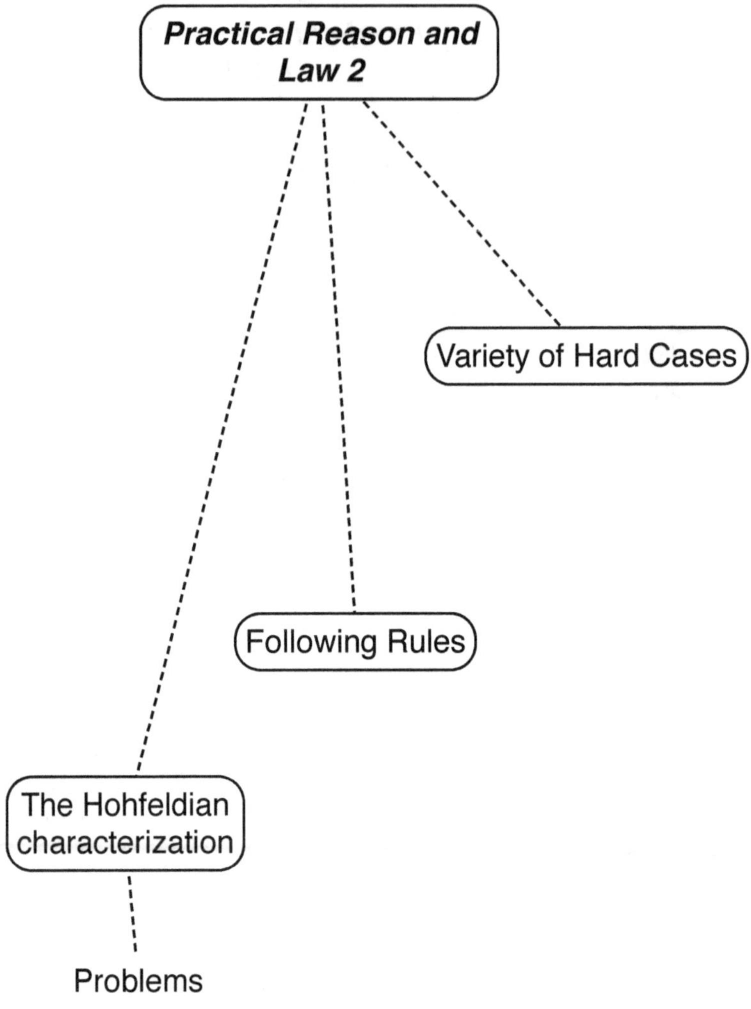
Practical Reason and Law 2
Variety of Hard Cases
Following Rules
The Hohfeldian characterization
Problems

10. Kelsen's Theory of Law: Norms and Delicts

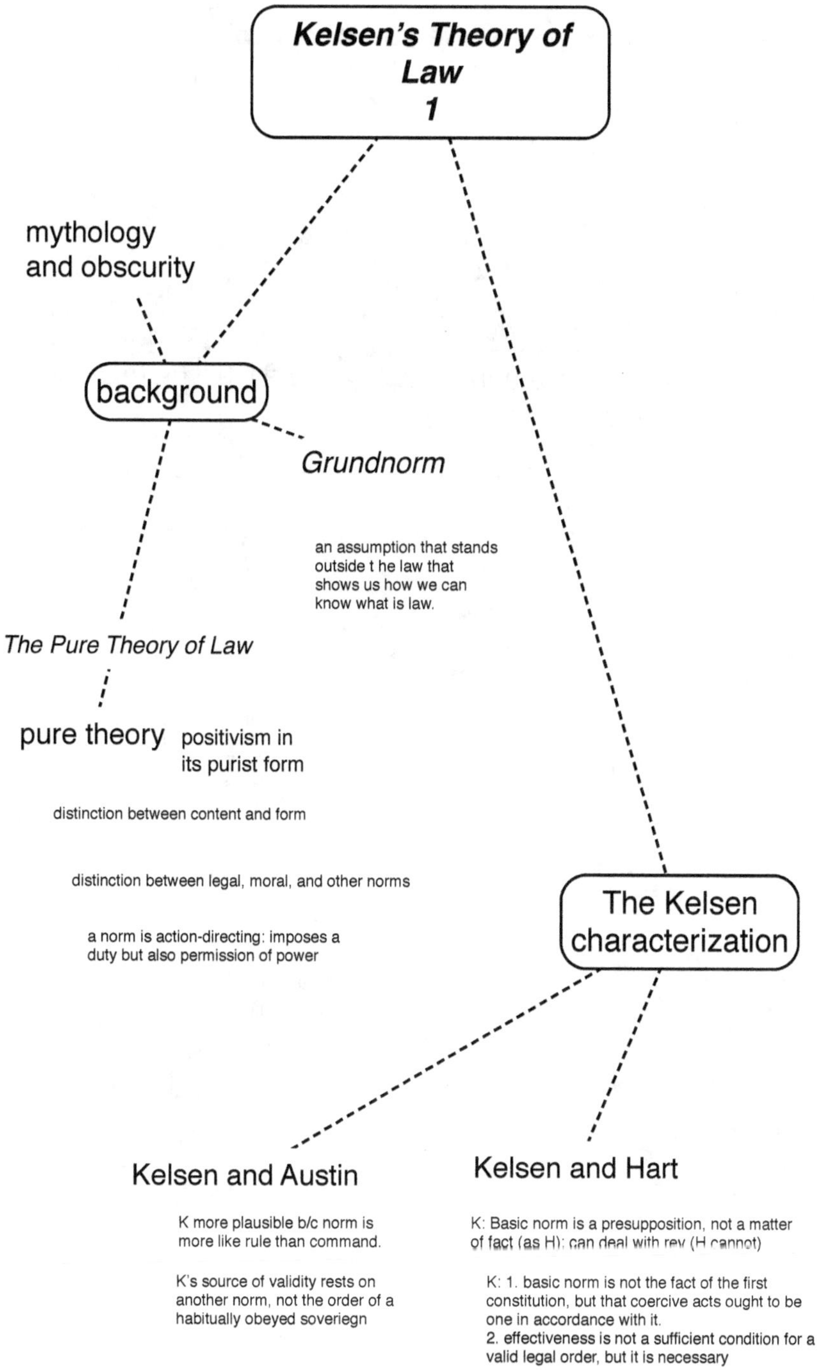

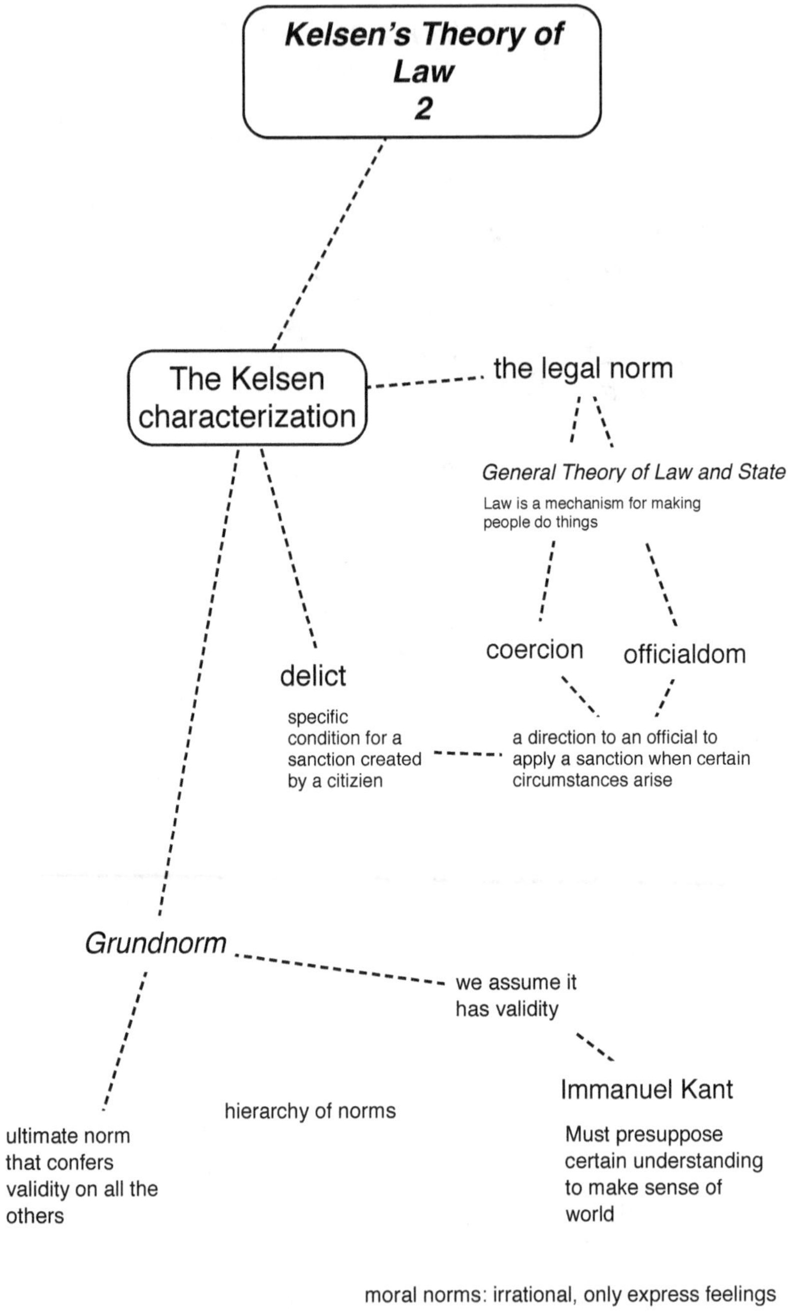
Kelsen's Theory of Law 2
The Kelsen characterization
the legal norm
General Theory of Law and State
Law is a mechanism for making people do things
coercion
officialdom
delict
specific condition for a sanction created by a citizien
a direction to an official to apply a sanction when certain circumstances arise
Grundnorm
we assume it has validity
Immanuel Kant
Must presuppose certain understanding to make sense of world
ultimate norm that confers validity on all the others
hierarchy of norms
moral norms: irrational, only express feelings

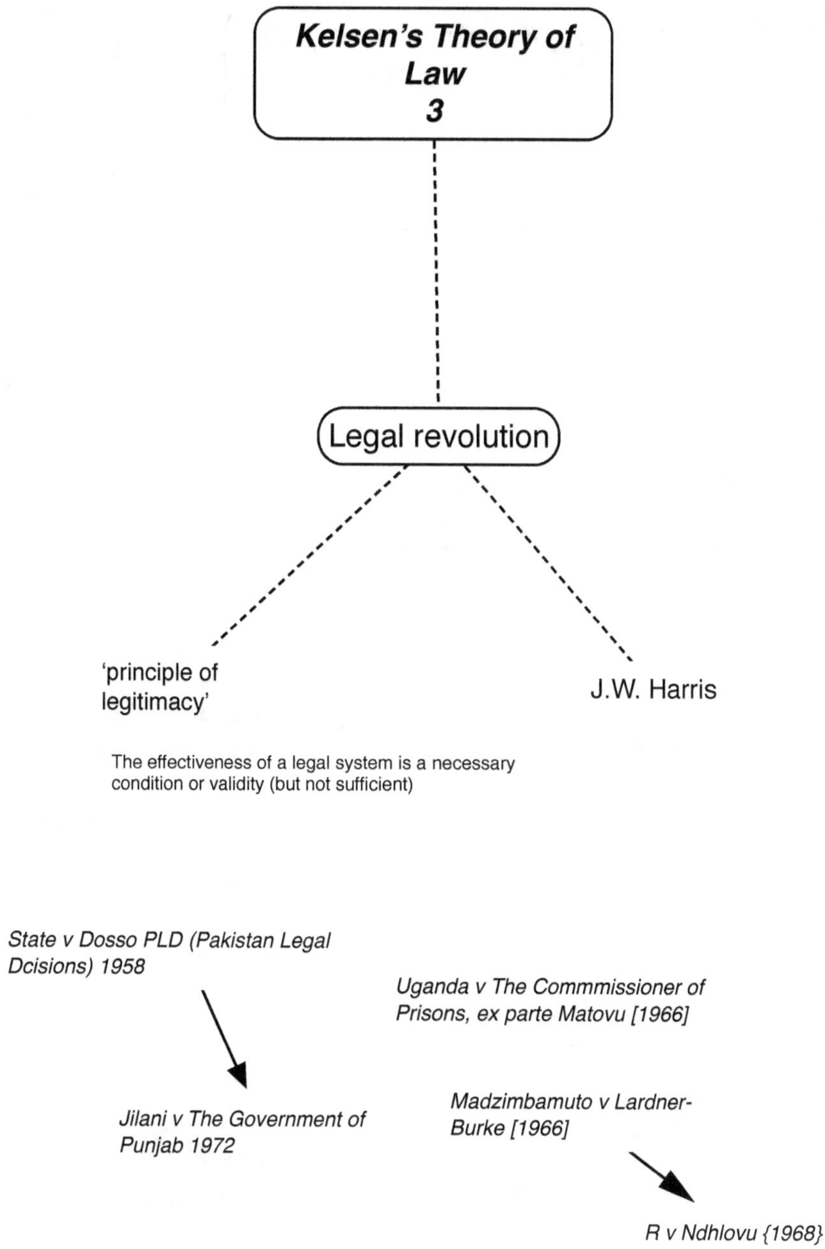
Kelsen's Theory of Law 3
Legal revolution
'principle of legitimacy'
J.W. Harris
The effectiveness of a legal system is a necessary condition or validity (but not sufficient)
State v Dosso PLD (Pakistan Legal Dcisions) 1958
Jilani v The Government of Punjab 1972
Uganda v The Commmissioner of Prisons, ex parte Matovu [1966]
Madzimbamuto v Lardner-Burke [1966]
R v Ndhlovu {1968}

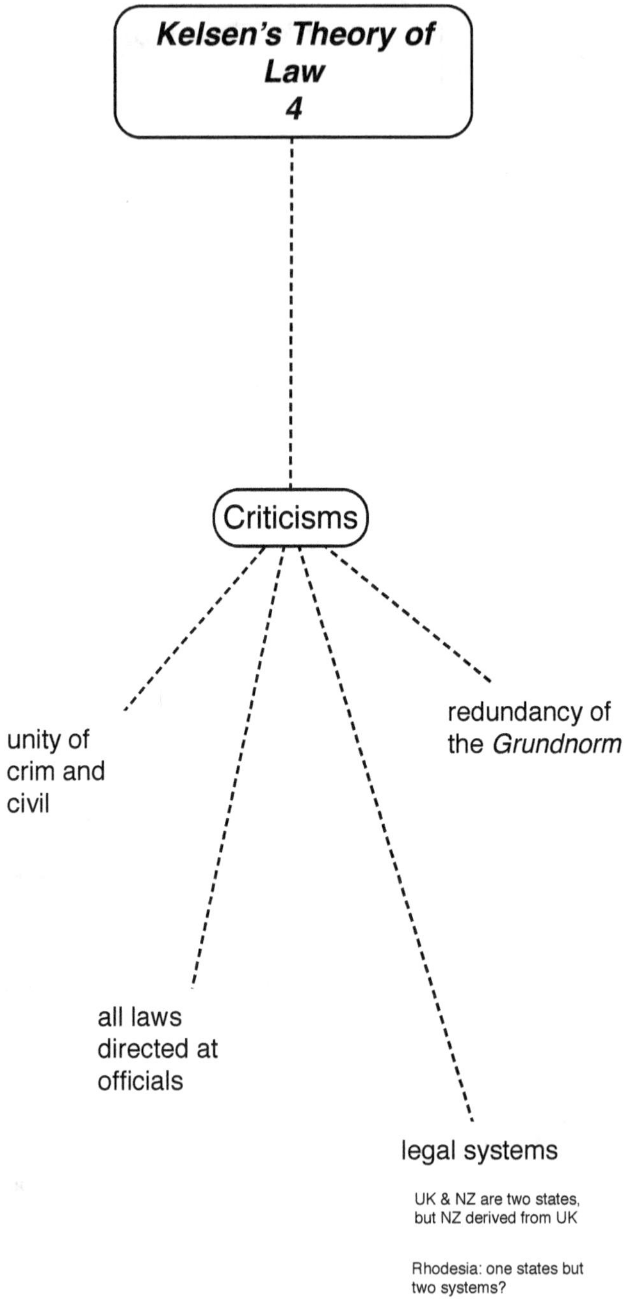
Kelsen's Theory of Law 4
Criticisms
unity of crim and civil
all laws directed at officials
legal systems
UK & NZ are two states, but NZ derived from UK
Rhodesia: one states but two systems?
redundancy of the Grundnorm

11. Dworkin's Theory of Law

Integrity and Interpretation of Law 1

Idea of Interpretation

Definition

making the best best of, its point
Like artistic interpet
Unlike scientific interp
unlike conversational interp

more than just describing
connection between law and morality is interpretive

Analytic attitudes

pre-interp, interp, post-interp

Judge Hercules

Accepts settled practice
Therefore accepts some gen'l political theory
Hard cases, accepts most of settled rules

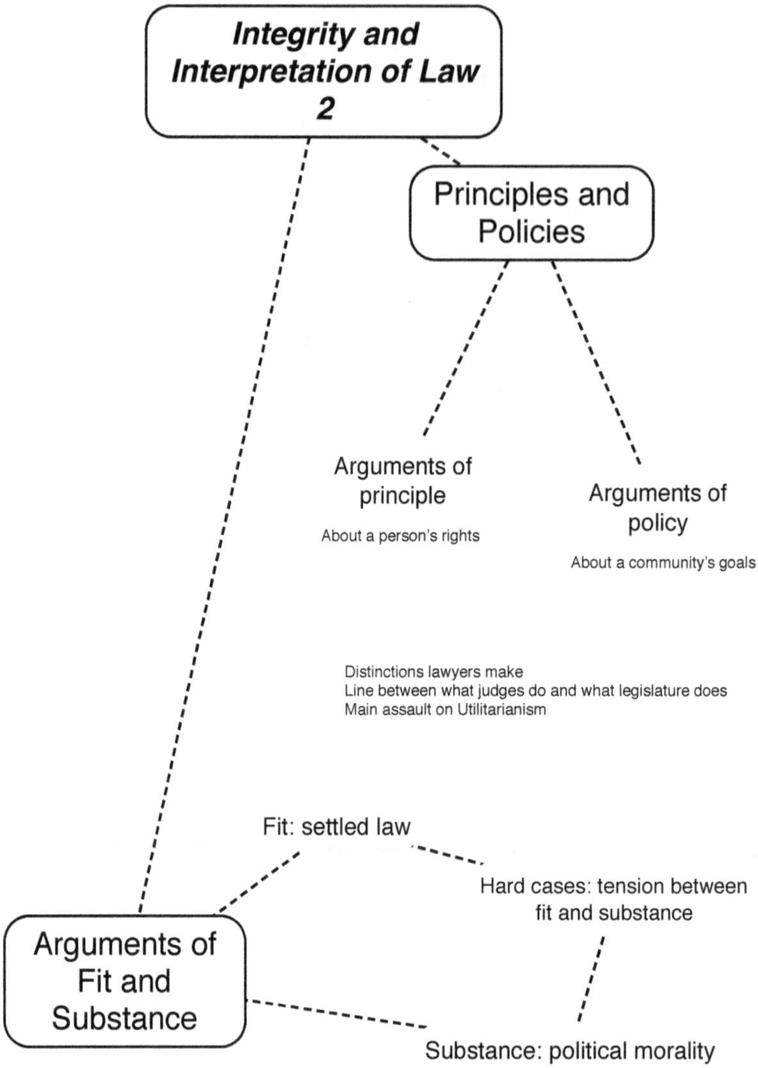

McLoughlin v O'Brian

Six possible interpretations:
1. only where physical injury (does not fit law of tort, no fit)
2. emotion injury occurs at accident (draws arbitrary moral line)
3. economically efficient (gov policy not principle, irrelevant to P's rights)
4. only where direct consequence of accident (contrary to fit-contradicts case law foreseeablity-no fit)
*5. Where injury is foreseeable
*6. where foreseeable, except when unfair financial burden on prerson who caused accident

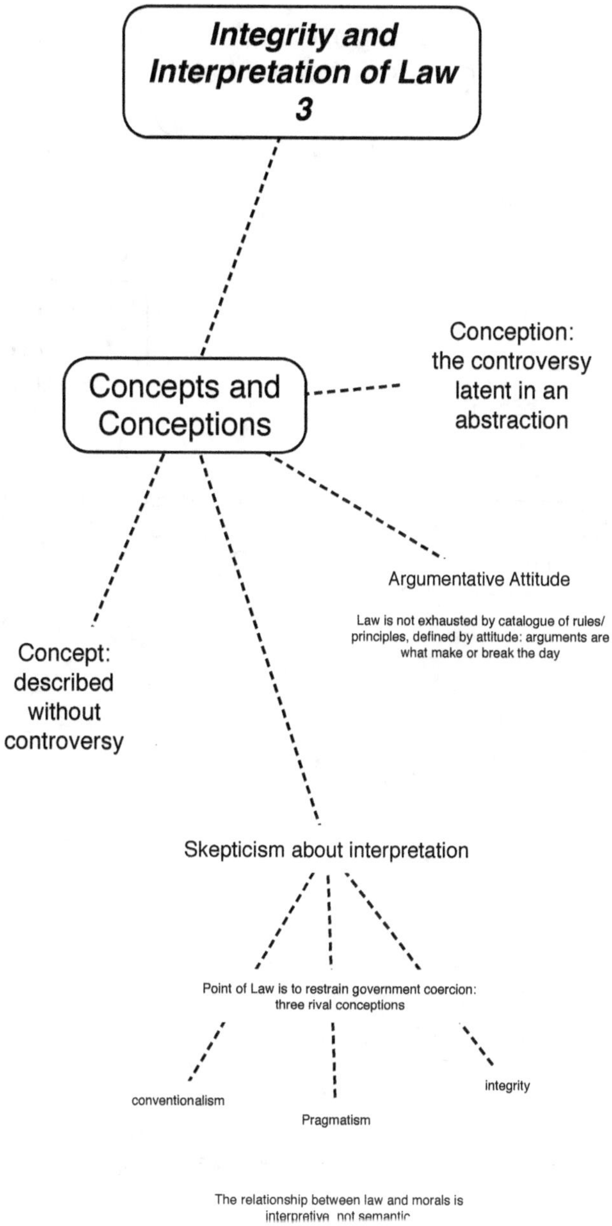
Integrity and
Interpretation of Law
3
Concepts and
Conceptions
Conception:
the controversy
latent in an
abstraction
Argumentative Attitude
Law is not exhausted by catalogue of rules/
principles, defined by attitude: arguments are
what make or break the day
Concept:
described
without
controversy
Skepticism about interpretation
Point of Law is to restrain government coercion:
three rival conceptions
conventionalism
Pragmatism
integrity
The relationship between law and morals is
interpretive, not semantic

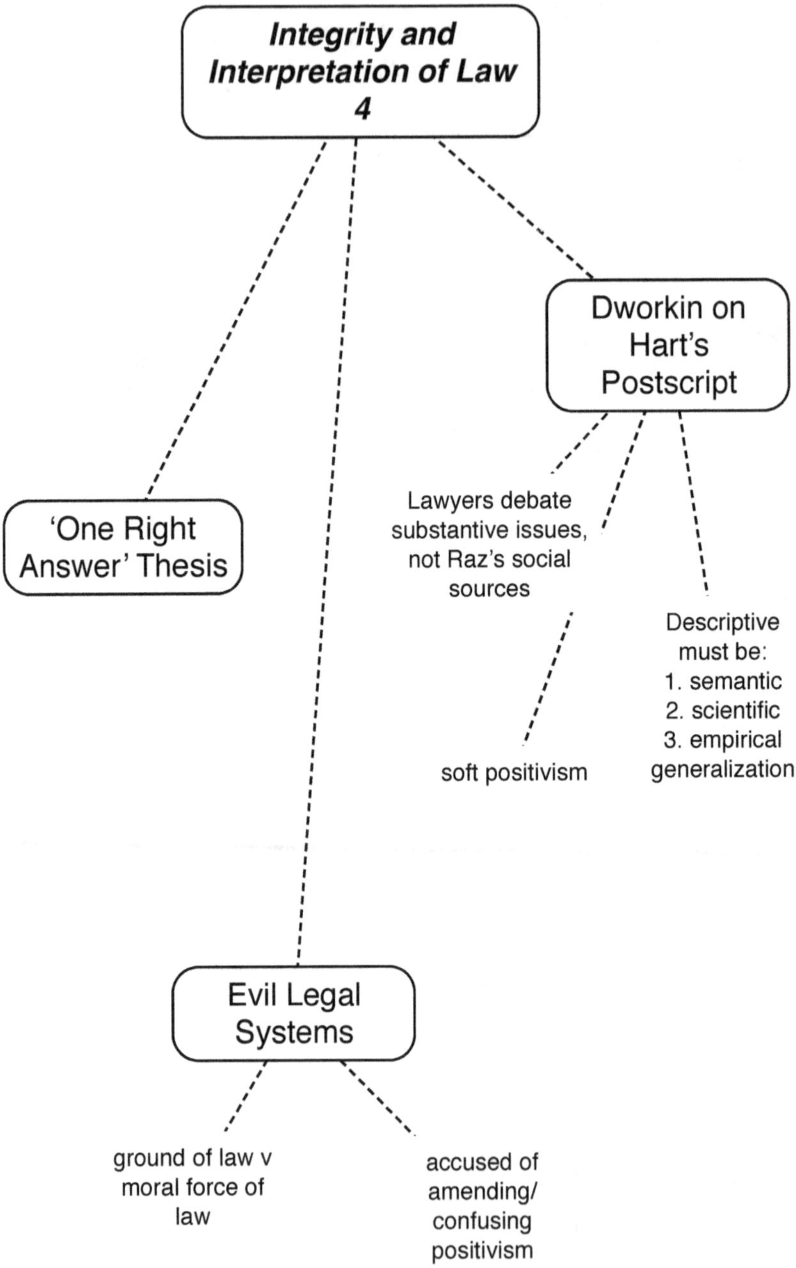
Integrity and Interpretation of Law 4
'One Right Answer' Thesis
Dworkin on Hart's Postscript
Lawyers debate substantive issues, not Raz's social sources
soft positivism
Descriptive must be:
1. semantic
2. scientific
3. empirical generalization
Evil Legal Systems
ground of law v moral force of law
accused of amending/ confusing positivism

12. Marxism and Marxist Legal Theory

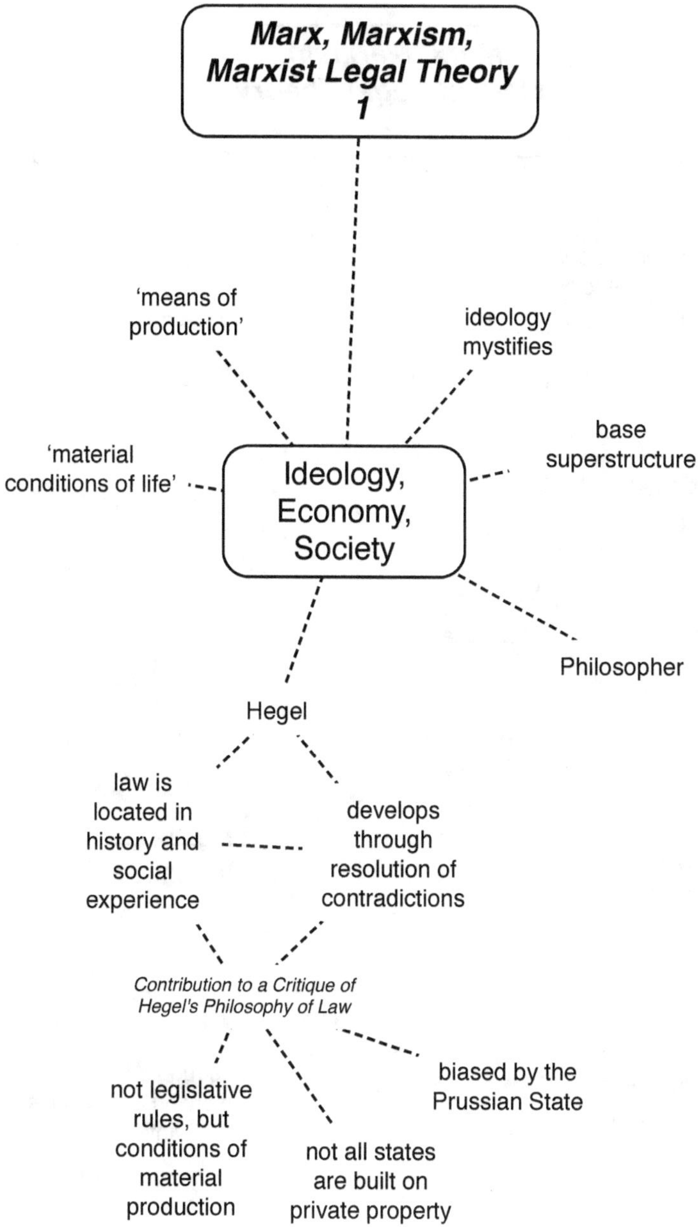

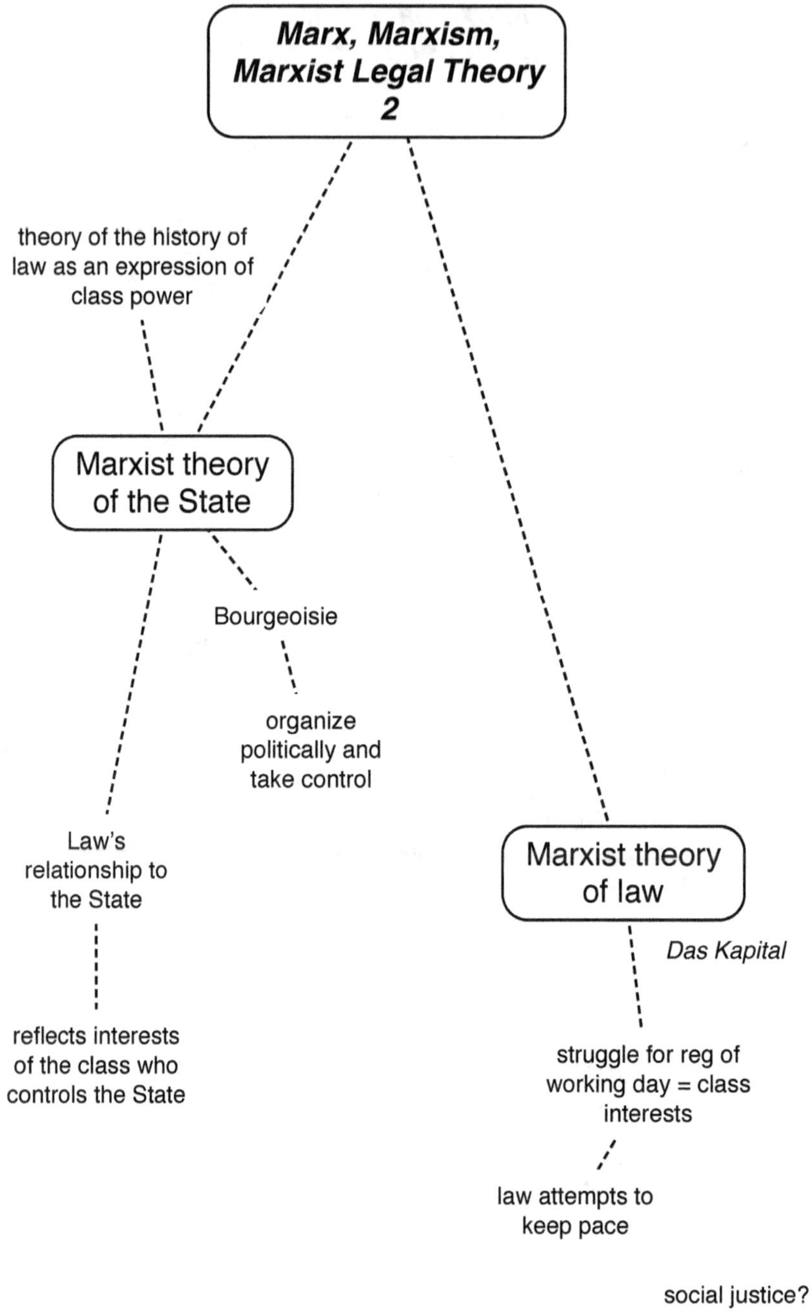
Marx, Marxism, Marxist Legal Theory 2
theory of the history of law as an expression of class power
Marxist theory of the State
Bourgeoisie
organize politically and take control
Law's relationship to the State
reflects interests of the class who controls the State
Marxist theory of law
Das Kapital
struggle for reg of working day = class interests
law attempts to keep pace
social justice?

Marx, Marxism, Marxist Legal Theory 3
Soviet Marxism and the Law
Russian Revolution 1917
Lenin
• communal ownership of the means of production
• a practical argument: B law swept away as relates to private ownership (a gradulaist approach)
Evgeny Pashukanis
• triumph of planned economy and destruction of private property
• contrasts capitalism with feudalism
• but how does law operate in society that has rejected the market?

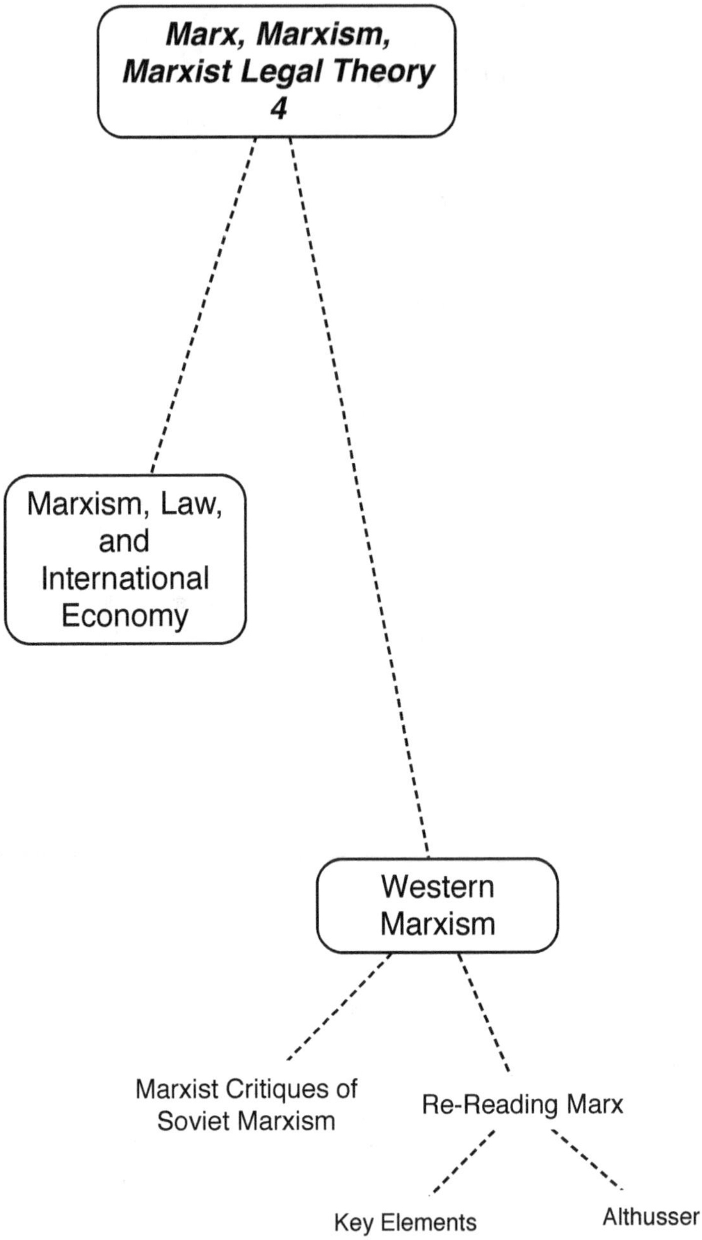
Marx, Marxism, Marxist Legal Theory 4
Marxism, Law, and International Economy
Western Marxism
Marxist Critiques of Soviet Marxism
Re-Reading Marx
Key Elements
Althusser

13. Liberalism

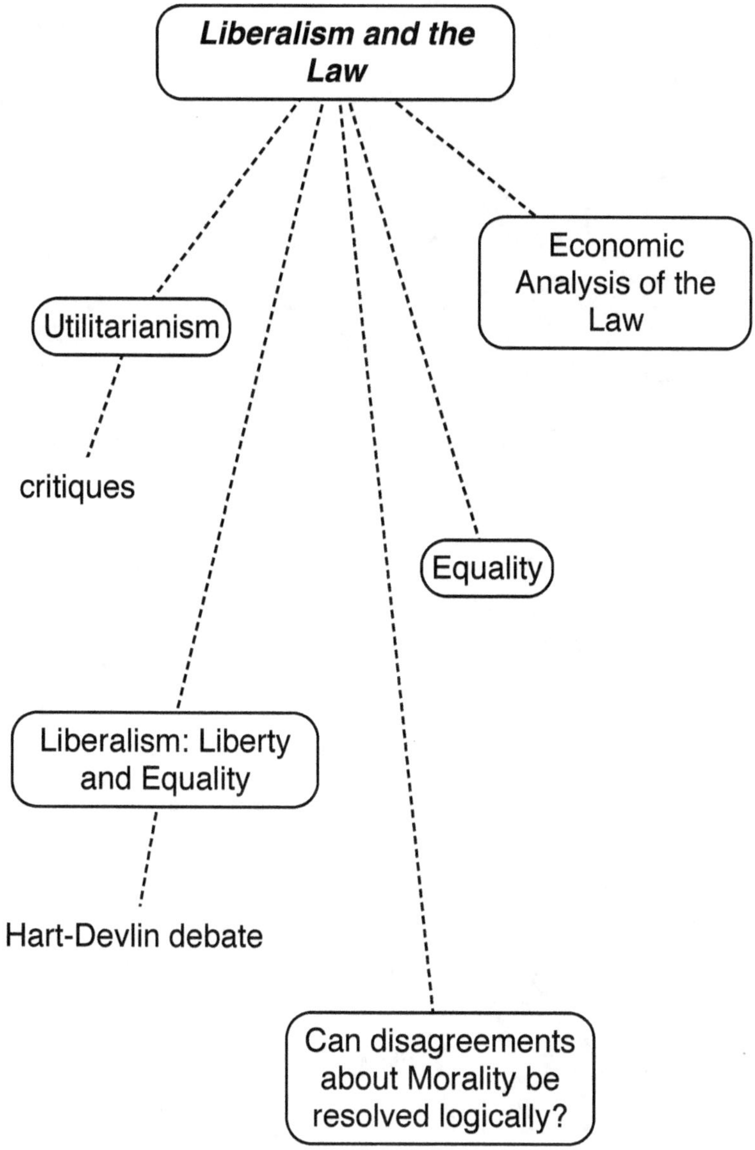

14. Feminist Legal Theory

Feminist Legal Theory 1

Brief History

Enlightenment Feminists

Mary Wollstonecraft

socialization

Suffragettes

equal protection under law

Second wave

civil rights movement
employment, reproductive rights

Third wave

Lacey

1st wave - Liberalists
2d wave - assert differences
3d - asks woman question

Feminist Legal Theory 2

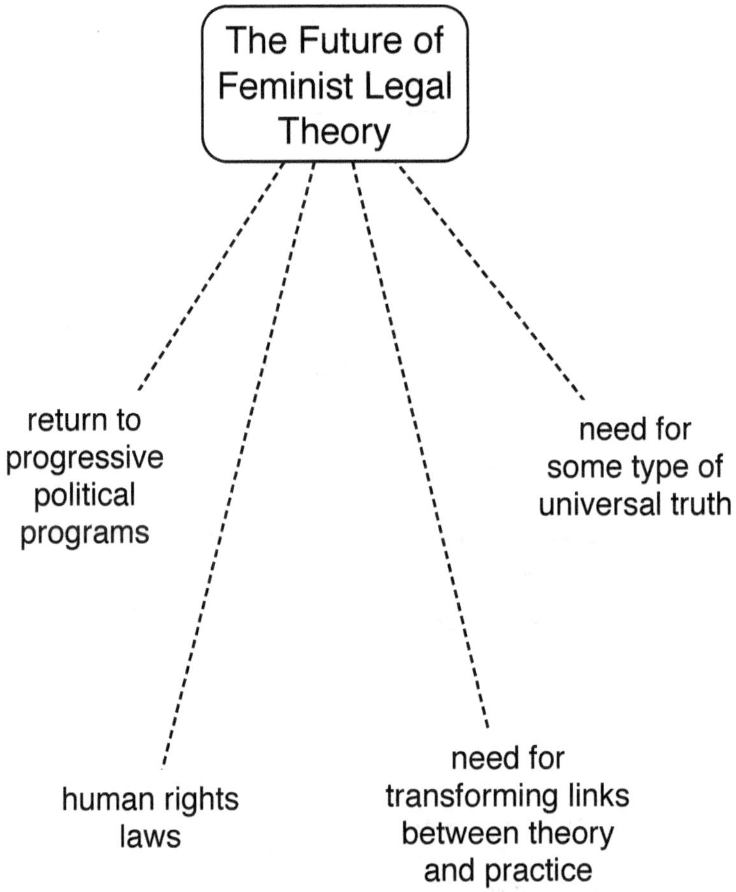

Feminist Legal Theory 3

pivotal event

The French Revolution

divorce laws

inheritance laws

political affairs

Destruction and reconstruction

2d wave = myths of universality

Feminist issues with the law

TACTICS
1. Women's injuries and actual harm

2. critique of epistemiology of law; relationship of jurisprudence to wider Western philosophical themes

Feminist Legal Theory 4

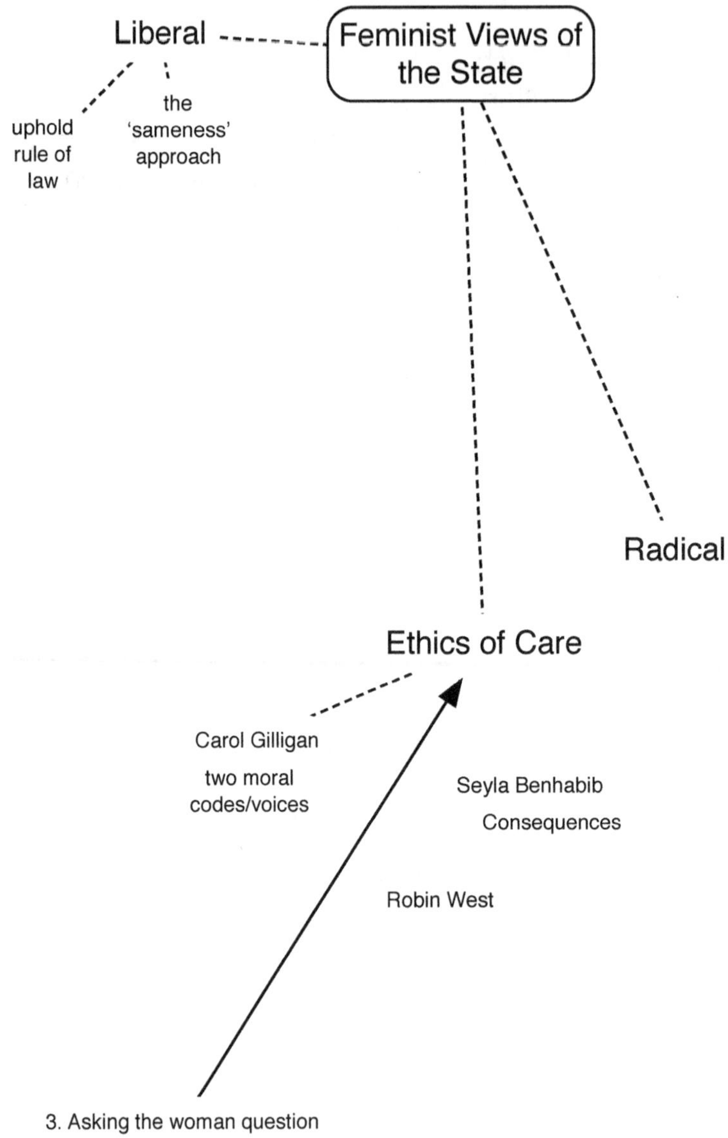

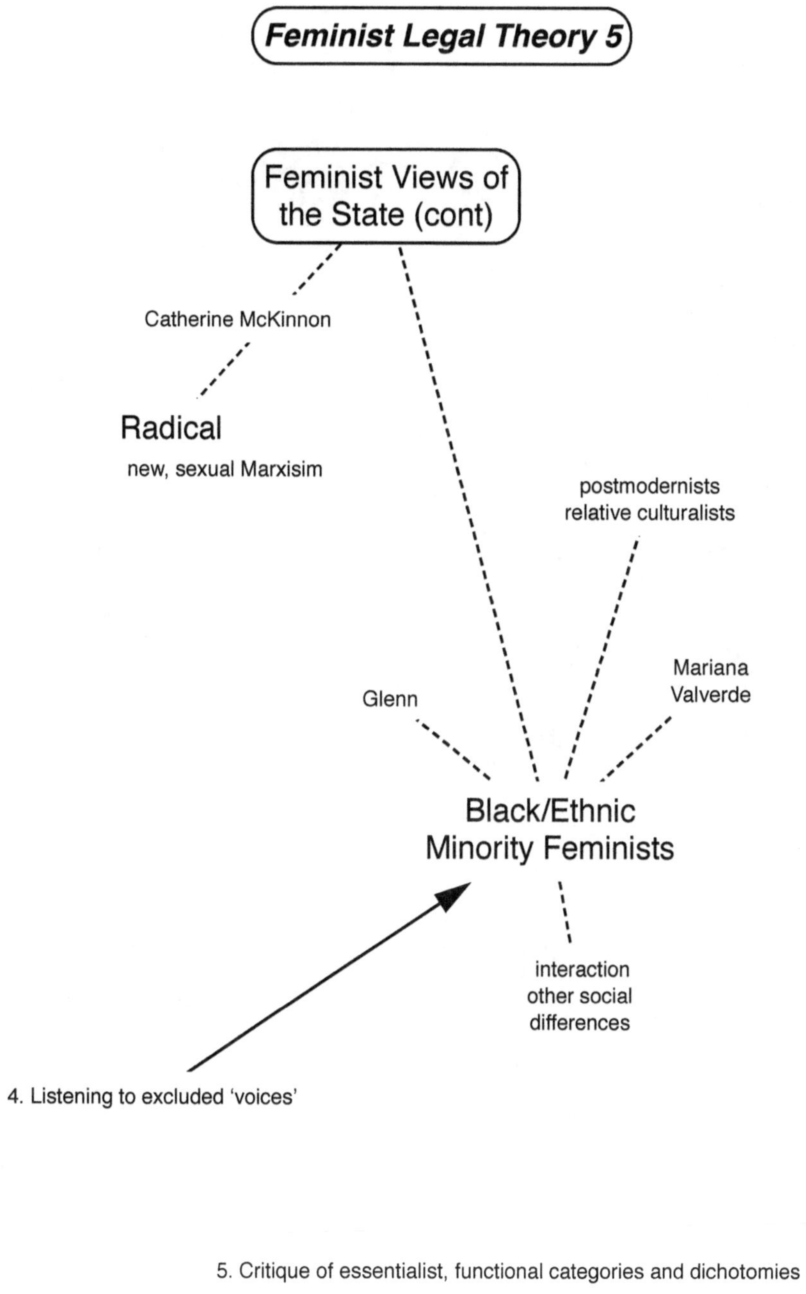
Feminist Legal Theory 5
Feminist Views of the State (cont)
Catherine McKinnon
Radical
new, sexual Marxisim
postmodernists
relative culturalists
Mariana
Valverde
Glenn
Black/Ethnic
Minority Feminists
interaction
other social
differences
4. Listening to excluded 'voices'
5. Critique of essentialist, functional categories and dichotomies

EXAM STUDY SHEETS

Exam Study Sheets are condensed outlines, based on the Course Outlines above. These are designed to help you get the "big picture" for revising and for testing yourself in preparation for exams. Each Exam Sheet contains 1–5 pages on each of the topics covered in the Course Outlines and Diagrams, including a few key statutes and cases for each.

Suggested study plan.

1. Look over the readings, Course Outlines, and Course Diagrams for the first topic.
2. Using the Exam Study Sheet for the first topic, test yourself on each item. Can you explain each one in detail? Can you remember important elements, discuss cases and statutes, and explain the concepts?
3. Review the Course outlines and Diagrams in areas where you are weak. Refer to your course materials to revise and review.
4. Repeat for each topic in the course.

When you are preparing for your exams, use the Exam Study Sheet as one of your tools for testing yourself.

2. The Nature of Legal Theory

2.1 Definitions

– Legal philosophy, political morality, sociology, and history.

– Various theories contribute to an understanding of how law works and how it should work.

– Help judges and lawyers think and approach the law as a whole.

2.2 Methodology, Analysis, Theory, Definition

– Descriptive and Normative theories

– A theory can be both

– A descriptive theory can address the normative:

2.3 Theory and Evaluation

– Finnis notes '…that the evaluation of theorist are an indispensable and decisive component in the selection or formation of any concepts for use in description of such aspects of human affairs such as law or legal order.' (*Natural Law and Natural Rights*, chapter 1).

– Hart chooses a wide conception of law over narrow one.

2.4 The 'Interpretive' Approach

– Concepts are a loosely defined and uncontroversial.

– D from 'conceptions'.

2.5 Summary

– Deep questions of methodology.

– List the various approaches of important scholars and movements.

– Give your own understanding and critiques of each theory, construction, approach.

3. Hobbes, Bentham, and Austin Imperative Theory (Command Theory)

3.1 Thomas Hobbes and the Beginnings of Positivism

- Founder of liberalism
- a reaction against medieval view of God was Creator.
- More secular approach to government, law, and society as human activities
- Father of legal positivism,
- *Leviathan*
  - The greatest enemy is social chaos;
  - The natural condition of humankind
  - This is the 'social contract.'

3.2 Jeremy Bentham

- Government is responsible to organize civil society and interaction (law)
- Goal was 'the greatest happiness of the greatest number is the foundation of morals and legislation.'
- 'Enlightened self-interest'

– The *panopticon.*

3.3 John Austin

– The 'command theory of law' .

– An ardent proponent of utilitarianism.

Lasting Contributions

– Analytical jurisprudence.

– Key concepts of law: right, duty, and legal validity.

– Law as object of scientific study

Command Theory

– Law is the creation of a sovereign (government)

– Commands

– Rules

– Sovereign

– Positive Law is contrasted with 'laws by close analogy' and 'laws by remote analogy'

Criticisms

– Hans Kelsen's 'pure' theory of law

– Identifying a 'sovereign'.

– New rulers.

– Does not fit some areas of law.

– Cannot distinguish between rules of terror and just rules.

4. Natural Law Theory

4.1 Ancient Greece and Rome

- The application of the theory of morality
  - A universal standard of justice for diverse people.
- Different natural law theories
- "Natural Law" definitions (ancient and modern)
- Influence and transmission of the ideas of Socrates, Plato, Aristotle, and the Stoics
- *lex injusta non est lex* ("an unjust law is not law").

4.2 Thomas Aquinas

- A classical natural law tradition incorporating Christian theology.
- Types of law
  - Eternal law.
  - Natural law.
  - Human law.
  - Divine law.

4.3 Divine Law, Human Law, and Obligation

- Laws reflect directly or indirectly the universal morality of natural law.
- Natural law (God) has two types of guidelines from which humans can reason:
  - *specificatio*:
  - *determinatio*:
- An overriding moral requirement to obey the law.

4.4 John Finnis and Modern Natural Law Theory

- Positivism is a partial theory or flawed theory.
- Two major arguments against natural law:
  - Moral skeptics
    - Moral realist.
    - Cognitivists
    - Emotivists
  - The fact/value distinction/the 'naturalistic fallacy' (G.E. Moore)
    - David Hume: cannot derive an 'ought' from an 'is'
- Natural Law theory says there *are* universal principles.
- Finnis: founded on man's ability to grasp fundamental values

    1. *life*
    2. *knowledge*
    3. *play*

4. *aesthetic experience*
5. *friendship*
6. *religion*
7. *practical reasonableness.*

– Not a utilitarian

4.5 Lon Fuller and Modern Natural Law Theory

– Criticized legal positivism.

– Secular natural law theory.

  – Moral content in the concept of 'the rule of law.'

  – Not a general moral theory

– A *procedural* natural law theory.

4.6 Summary

– The connection between law and morality is a large and complex area.

– Hart is sensitive to the arguments and tenants of natural law theory.

– Dworkin also saw connections between morality and law, but refuted positivism.

5. HLA Hart's: *The Concept of Law*

5.1 Overview

- A restatement the theory of legal positivism for the modern world.
- 'descriptive sociology' and 'analytical jurisprudence.'
- based on the modern municipal legal system.'
- Authorities accept the system as a matter of fact, so moral content is not necessary
- Criticizes the Command Theory (Chapters 2-4)
- Law is made up of a union between 'primary' and 'secondary rules' under the 'rule of recognition' (Chapter 5-6)
- Defends legal positivism against natural law (Chapter 9).
- Postscript: A reply to Ronald Dworkin's criticism.

5.2 The Aims of the Theory

- A descriptive theory of law'.

5.3 Definition and Theory

- Addresses three questions

1. What is the differences between law and coercion?
2. What is the relationship between legal obligation and moral obligation?
3. What does it mean to say that 'a social rule exists' in a particular society?

- Hart's 'model' of law, which allows difficult cases, international law, and primitive law to be addressed
- Model is a central set of elements, a union of primary and secondary rules, that describe the 'modern municipal legal system.'
- International law "is law to the extent that it shares similarities with the model, and not law to the extent that it does not."

5.4 Criticism of the Orders Backed By Threats Theory

- A standard accepted by at least some members of the group is better than the concepts of an order.
- Rules can refer to legal duties, powers, as well as standard laws.

5.5 The 'Union of Primary and Secondary Rules'

- The 'central set of elements' is the 'the union of primary and secondary rules.'
  - duty-imposing rules
  - power-conferring rules
  - three power-conferring rules
    - rules of change
    - rules of adjudication
    - the rule of recognition.

- The rule of recognition is accepted by the judges of the system as a fact.
- a legal system 'exists' is
  - essentially effective
  - rules of recognition are accepted as valid.

5.6 Legal Reasoning, Natural Law, International Law

- Chapter 7: Legal reasoning, 'core' and the 'penumbra' in 'settled' law, American Legal Realism
  - Chapter 8: Natural Law
  - Chapter 10: Summary and International Law

5.7 The 'Internal' Point of View

- The citizens and official accept the rules of the system *from inside* the system.
- Critiques
  - why should they?
  - Perry: the methodology is not purely neutral and descriptive.
  - May require a moral argument, and not just a descriptions, though that is his attempt.

7. Hart's Defenses Against Natural Law Theorists and Fuller

7.1 Morality

- American Realist adherents are wrong about morality and law
- does sometimes happen, but not always, and it does not have to.

7.2 The Nazi Grudge Informer

- The "Nazi Grudge Informer"
- Legal Positivism: grudge informer acted legally, though also immorally.
- Natural Law theory: just because that the action was immoral, no legal defense, because the law was immoral (against nature).
- Positivism makes more sense of the situation.
- Positivism is justified in practice because it results in a morally better result.
  - (contradicts his argument that there is no moral bias in his theory?)

7.3 Fuller's Principles of the 'Inner Morality' of the Law

- Fuller: evil endeavors do not operate logically, but moral endeavors do.
- If law is logically and rationally structured, it can be moral.
- The Eight principles of the 'inner morality of law'
    1. be promulgated
    2. not be retroactive
    3. be general
    4. be clear
    5. not be inconsistent
    6. not require the impossible
    7. be congruent with official action
    8. be reasonably stable
- Hart's criticism: easy to come up with 'eight principles' of anything

6. Hart's Rule of Recognition

6.1 *Identifying the Rule*

- Functions to identify the law of a particular system.
  - The 'ultimate rule'
  - contains 'supreme' and 'subordinate' criteria of legal validity.
- Crucial in defining a legal system.
  - whether or not another rule is part of the legal system.
  - An empirical fact
  - Often not stated.
- The 'Supreme Criterion'.
- The ultimate rule is the Rule of Recognition itself.
  - Kelsen's *Grundnorm*
- Makes a distinction between the Supreme Criterion and Rule of Recognition. (contra Austin)

The Validity of a Legal System

- Officials in the system accept the Rule of Recognition
- Generally obeyed by both officials and private citizens.

6.2 Criticisms

- Finnis criticizes Hart's rule of recognition
  - Too much emphasis on its identification through empirical fact
  - Moral evaluation required?
  - how are officials are to view the Rule of Recognition?
  - a central set of elements?
  - must be a *moral* acceptance of the rule
- Dworkin criticizes the Rule of Recognition
  - No judicial reasoning outside of law
  - Cannot adequately justify the law to be applied.
  - any rule which cannot be identified with certainty is not a rule of law at all
    - Means If it is controversial, it is not a law, judge must legislate
    - retrospective legislation!
  - Hart's is misdescribing what judges do and say they do
  - Because a major part of the law involves legal *argument*, positivism fails as a model
  - (But Hart did distinguish between 'core' meanings and 'penumbras'.)
- Finnis' and Dworkin's arguments:
  - legal theory must explain the moral force of law;
  - proper operation of law requires making the best *moral* sense of the existing practices.

6.3 The Postscript

- Legal theory involves a descriptive account of the concept of law.
- Denies legal theory is interested in justification—he is only describing.
- Affirms evil legal systems are law.

The Hart and Dworkin Debate

- The postscript is Hart's counter to Dworkin's attack on legal positivism.
- Hart: both descriptive *and* general, no particular legal system.
  - morally neutral.
- Dworkin attempts evaluate and justify a particular legal system.
- Not guilty of "semantic sting"
  - (Yet chapters 1-4?)
  - makes choices between theories and concepts
- Nazi legal system was valid law, even if morally bankrupt
- Hart concerned about *universal*; Dworkin about *justification* (two different things)

Principles and the Rule of Recognition

- Dworkin too sharp a distinction between rules and principles.
- Wrong about *Riggs v Palmer*

Judicial Discretion

- Dworkin thinks that judicial law-making is a threat to democracy; Hart does not
- Hart says the application of retrospective legislation in hard cases doesn't matter

8. Raz's Theory of Law: Service Conception

8.1 The Paradox of Authority and the 'Service' Conception of Authority

– The 'paradox of authority': makes no sense to follow authority

– The argument against: society would be worse off without.

– Hobbes: legitimacy of a state was found in a 'social contract'

– Others: authorities know more than a regular citizen does

– The 'service conception' of authority.

8.2 The 'Normal Justification Theory'

– "normal justification" theory addresses the authority paradox.

The Balance of Reasons

– i.e., choosing to go to a doctor rather than diagnose and treat yourself

– An authority (such as a doctor) serves you ('service conception') by helping you balance the reasons.

The Normal Justification Thesis

- Legal authorities mediate this balance
- A legislature considers and debates, passes a law.
- Authority gains legitimacy when it mediates these issues

The Scope of Authority

- Over some areas, not others.
- Some see this as a flaw in Raz's theory

8.3 Exclusionary Reasons

-Authorities do their work in two stages:

- Deliberative Reasoning
  - Executive Reasoning.
- results of Decision-making bodies are taken as exclusionary reasons
- demonstrates that authorities are an important part of practical reasoning.
- meaningful because they have thought through the 'balance of reasons'

Force and Scope of the Reasons

- 'Exclusionary reasons' stand on their own (as authoritative).
- Exclusionary reasons are about actions, not thinking about them.
- Exclusionary reasons have scope.

8.4 The Authority and Scope of Law

- The law claims the authority to make rules
- The expects people to follow the rules.
- The law mediates between the balance of reasons and it citizens.
- The process of the making of authoritative laws is well-structured
  - It deliberates and then issues an order (law, ruling).
  - The order cannot be authoritative if it does not mediate between the balance of reasons
  - The orders must be specific enough to give direction
  - If the order is not specific, then it cannot be ordered.

8.5 Soft Positivism

- An order has authority if it is possible to follow it
  - on its own terms
  - without need for further deliberation.
- Laws which refer to anything 'morality requires' are not authoritative
  - are really orders that give judges the power to make specific orders or law in specific cases.
- All legal systems seem to contain laws of this kind; therefore, all legal systems give judges this power
  - Supports Hart's claim.
  - Dworkin disagrees

9. Practical Reason and the Law

9.1 Definitions

– Norm

– Rule

– Order

– Rights

– Powers

– Duties: exclusionary reasons (in Raz's terms).

9.2 Norms

– Standards of behavior that people are expected to follow.

– Rules, rights, duties, and powers

– Rights can be

  – *in rem*

  – *in personam*,

– The "choice" or "will" theory of rights

– The "interest" theory of rights

9.3 Hohfeld's Theory of Legal Norms

- Followed early American Realist theories
- Theory focuses on what courts do
- Criticism: does not really reflect how these concepts work out in the legal field.

9.4 Rule-Following

- Hart's practical theory of rules is criticized for:
  - not distinguishing between rules and reasons that are generally accepted
  - for not being able to define the normativity of rules, which does not depend on a practice of them.
- Wittgenstein's argument about rule-following.

9.5 Hard Cases

- The classical concept of 'equity' is often applied in such cases;
  - But the classic saying, "hard cases make bad law."
- when subjective concepts of law must be employed.
- If two or more laws conflict
- If two or more difficult laws could reasonably underlie a series of cases or a statute.
- Rules can be interpreted in different ways by different judges.

10. Kelsen's Theory of Law: Norms and Delicts

10.1 Overview

- A continental form of Legal Positivism.
- Law could be identified purely by its form rather than content
- define action-directing rules of behavior (norms) which either places duties on people or give them powers.
    - objective task.
    - Morality is a subjective opinion.
- An important term: *Grundnorm*

10.2 The **Grundnorm** *and Delicts*

- Kelsen's theory takes the point of view of those in power.
- Citizen commit 'delicts'.
- Officials are to apply sanctions when a delict is committed
- All valid laws rest on a higher norm or law, eventually reaching the the *Grundnorm* .
    - (Contra Austin and Hart)
- effectiveness of a system is a necessary condition.

The Legal Norm

– Law used to 'order human behaviour'

– power to authorities to use sanctions in certain situations and times.

– 'Coercion' and 'officialdom'.

– A 'legal norm'.

– Criticism: most people think law is directed at the citizens.

The Delict

– 'if someone commits a delict, then the official should impose the relevant sanction.

– Admits it is to think of laws as directed at citizens.

– Delict places an obligation on the authority; only officials can break the law.

The Basic Norm (the *Grundnorm)*

– As one moves up the chain of validity of each law, the highest law is the ultimate norm

– the ultimate norm because it is assumed so by the system.

Austin

– More sound than Austin's because a norm is more like a rule than a command.

– Idea of a norm works better because it can distinguish between 'being obliged' from being 'under obligation' which OBT cannot

- *Grundnorm* makes more sense than resting it on a person or a group (Autin's habitually-obeyed 'sovereign')

Hart

- basic norm is a presupposition of the ultimate authority, rather than a matter of fact (Hart).
- Presuppositon of a revolution regime could simply be ignored (could not happen in Hart's theory
- It is not a *fact* of the first constitution, as Hart would say, it is the presupposed norm.
- Effectiveness is not a *sufficient condition*, but it is a *necessary* condition.
  - (Hart believes it is sufficient)

10.3 Legal Revolutions

- A full-scale revolution where a new government introduced a new constitution would
  - Need to be effective.
  - old laws would not longer be valid.
  - But new regime is not automatically valid.
  - It is *effective* but not yet *sufficient*

Theory of Revolution in the Real World

- *State v Dosso PLD* (Pakistan Legal Decisions) 1958
- *Ugandu v The Commissioner of Prisons, ex parte Matovu* [1966] with a similar decision.

- *Madzimbamuto v Lardner-Burke* [1966]

10.4 Criticisms

- Treats civil and criminal law together.
- Not how most people understand how the law works.
- Most people do not think of their system of law changing every time there is a change that does not fall under the presupposed norm (constitution).
- Raz: 'justified normatively' approach does not work.
- Hart makes the same point in *The Concept of Law*

11. Dworkin's Theory of Law

11.1 Interpretation and Practice

– law is best understood through its practice.

– figure out what would be the best sense of that practice

– 'constructive' or 'artistic interpretation'.

  – not 'scientific interpretation'

  – not 'conversational interpretation'.

Definition of 'Interpretation'

– Describe a legal practice 'at its best'.

– assume that it has a purpose.

Types of Attitudes Towards the Law

– *pre-interpretive*

– *interpretive*

– *Post-Interpretive.*

11.2 Judge Hercules

- Some have criticized the technique by saying no such judges exists,
- Model an *ideal* judge, against which good and bad legal arguments can be judged.
- Accepts the settled practice and general political theory of the legal system.
- In hard cases, he accepts and employs the settled rules
- He understands the theories that support the rules.
  - theory of responsibility in criminal law
  - theory of relevance in law of evidence
  - theory of division of capital and income in law of taxation
  - theory of consideration in law of contract

11.3 Principles and Policies

- Arguments about principles are arguments about rights.
- Arguments about legal policy are about reaching the goals a community sets for itself.
- For Dworkin, these two areas are crucial to distinguish
- Thisi is how Dworkin's attacks Utilitarianism.

11.4 'Fit' and 'Substance'.

- judges should not attempt to legislate
- judge's decisions should be in concert with present, accepted, received law

- In difficult cases, a judge should attempt to resolve in in a way that results in 'equality of respect'

Example of *McLoughlin v O'Brien*

--Dworkin suggested six possible ways to interpret and apply settled rules:

- Liable only where physical injury
  - Emotional injury can only occur at the accident
  - Economically efficient
  - Where the injury was a direct consequence of accident
  - Where the injury is foreseeable
  - Where the injury is foreseeable, except when it would place an unfair financial burden on the defendant

11.5 Concepts, Conceptions, Argumentation

- Distinction between conceptions and concepts
  - Pragmatism problem.
  - Conventionalism problem.
- 'Integrity' makes the best sense:

Skepticism and Truth

- A significant challenge to any interpretation
- 'global internal skepticism' must be skeptical of the theories of interpretation of law
- Law exists to restrain government

– Conventionalism

– Pragmatism

– Integrity

– Relationship between law and morality is interpretative.

The Argumentative Attitude

– Law is not just a bunch of rules, it is an attitude.

– Demonstrated in courtrooms.

11.6 The 'One Right Answer' Thesis

– Dworkin has no such a theory

– (though some accuse him of trying to develop one)

11.7 Evil Legal Systems

– Makes distinction between:

– The ground of law.

– The moral force of the law.

– Hart: merely adding to positivism or coming up with a 'confused' version.

– Dworkin's argument against this is complex.

11.8 Hart's Postscript

– Dworkin believes there *are* right answers to both legal and moral questions

- Makes no sense to say, without a doubt, that evil legal systems cannot be 'law'.
- Dworkin doesn't follow natural law.
- Some accuse him of being a sort of positivist, but Dworkin says he is not.
- Dworkin argues that without locating the *point* of finding law with a social source, it is not possible to find that source.
- Hart claims that moral principles *can* be part of the law ('soft positivism').
- Dworkin's three ways in which a legal theory might be called descriptive:
    - Isemantic description.
    - natural kind or type for law (as in science)
    - an empirical generalization
- 'Soft positivists' see social sources as the best way to identifying law (as opposed to Rax and 'hard' or 'exclusive' positivism).
    - Dworkin argues that this approach is hollow
    - also argues that it is not clear how legal positivist can assume that propositions about the sources are somehow different from other kinds of propositions.
- Dworkin characterizes that the approach of legal positivism as descriptive.

12. Marxism and Marxist Legal Theory

12.1 Ideology, Economy, and Society

- Theory of society and law based on analysis and critiques of Martin Hegel's theories.
- A materialistic understanding of social institutions (like law) as a way to understand the social economic context of them.

- Later became a political ideology that and movement.

Marx

- Marx was a philosopher.
- Marx: law was not part of philosophy that examined the 'development of the human mind'.
- Instead, law should be examined in terms of the 'material conditions of life'
- Law only one part of the social and political structure.
- The 'means of production' was Marx's term for this structure (which encompassed production, distribution, and exchange).
- The ideology of any group determines what they believe about their role, their society, and their values.
  - independence can be lost.
  - an instrument of class power.

Marx's Critique of Hegel

- Hegel: law was located in history and social experience
- Marx: the division of labor and classes comes from the conditions of material production.

Marx's Contribution

- Not all states are built on the concept and ground of private property
- Law is part of a larger system
- The form of law in any given system is determined by its historical and material circumstances.
- Law is not grounded in legislative rules, but the conditions of material production
- Marx describes how capital takes on a judicial form.

12.2 Theory of the State

- Those who own property control the State
- The State (and law) reflects the best interest of that class.
- justice and equality reflect the interests of that class
- legal theory is an expression of class power.

12.3 Theory of Law

- Those in power use the system to exploit those the other classes.
  - Social justice comes only through a transformation of the economic system.

- The movement to regulate the working day was fostered by class interests and struggles.
- The legal system and its laws attempted (and still attempt) to keep up with changes in society and technology social.
- The creation of the 'normal' working day is the result of a 'civil war' between the capitalist class and the working-class
- Social justice could only be achieved through a revolution.

12.4 Soviet Marxism

- The Russian Revolution of 1917.
  - problems and dissolution of the Soviet Union means there was something incorrect about Marxism.
- Lenin:
  - The laws set up by the bourgeoisie must be destroyed where it relates to ownership of private property.
  - A more gradual approach.
- Pashukanis
  - A planned economy
  - The destruction of private property
  - law could cease to function.
  - Criticism: how can law operate in a society with no market economy.

12.5 Western Marxism

- Althusser is good example

- person as a social being and how they relate to the economy.
- More sophisticated theory

12.6 Marxism and International Law

- Issues of class and larger global power structures.
- Baran
  - How wealth was transferred from the colonized nations and the Commonwealth to Western European nations.
  - agricultural nations were forced to serve the developed economies of the 'colonial masters'.
- Wallerstein
  - 'worlds systems theory'
  - world economy is result of the geographic expansions of Western countries beginning in the 16th century.
- Others
  - concepts of social justice on an international scale should not be the focus of law
  - too narrow a way to regulate global markets.

13. Liberalism

13.1 Utilitarian Approach

- A moral theory
- Bentham
- growth of English and Commonwealth society, the growth of liberalism, and current economics practices and theory.
- encompasses more than law
- many variations.
- Critics misunderstand how refined its application can be.

13.2 Criticisms of Utilitarianism

- The primary criticism: focuses too much on good of the whole; ignores individuals.
- Ignores *individual* rights.

13.3 Liberty and Equality as Liberal Concepts

- 'liberty' and 'equality' concepts.
- Both rooted in 'morality' or moral thinking.

– Lord Devlin and the 'man on the Clapham omnibus'

– Hart: does not believe that what the ordinary person thinks is grounded in 'moral rightness'

13.4 Approaches to Morality

– Dworkin outlines the concept of a moral position

  – irrational, prejudiced, a gut-reaction, or mere parroting.

– Glover

  – Moral arguments can be based on facts or not

  – Must get back to 'ultimate axioms'.

– Both: moral arguments are not *just* subjective opinions.

– Every argument or viewpoint could be a moral one (even if not valid).

13.5 Equality

– Equality could be seen in how we treat others, rather than on some scale

– This approach sees people as individuals and treating them 'fairly'.

13.6 Economics of Law Approach

– The Chicago School of Law'.

– Used Kaldor-Hicks criterion (rather than Pareto efficiency model)

– utilitarian approach—maximum efficiency of the system.

– Criticism: allocation must necessarily come before a judicial decision is rendered.

14. Feminist Legal Theory

14.1 Deconstruction and Reconstruction

- Feminist jurisprudence analyzes and critiques how law and a legal system supports division and hierarchy regarding gender.
- Seek to change the more oppressive divisions for women in subcultural, cultural, and global areas.
- Some of the approaches
  - injuries and harm to women are often dismissed as trivial, humorous, self-induced, biological, etc.
  - Critiquing approach and assumptions of traditional jurisprudence.
  - Critiquing 'abstract masculinity'
  - Gilligan
    - what it considered 'normal' has been organized by male thinking.
    - equality laws are really just trying to make women more like men.
  - analyze voices that have traditionally been excluded
  - critique of dualistic models

The French Revolution

- The event and its aftermath made the concepts of liberalism part of social reality.
  - creation of divorce laws
  - changing of inheritance laws.
  - issue of equal status of women in political affairs.
- Scott and Pateman:
  - goals of feminism will not be reached through the ideas of liberal political theory,
- Hunt
  - traditional political life: 'rational, public, and universal'.
  - women excluded because considered irrational, private, and particular-oriented.

14.2 History of Feminist Legal Theory

- Wollstonecraft
  - Argued that although women could reason.
  - remedied by changing the socialization patterns for children.
- 'Suffragettes' of the 20th Century (First Wave)
  - Primary: secure the right to vote for women (and other rights).
- The modern women's liberation movement (the 1960s and later) (Second Wave)
  - from civil rights movements
  - Sought freedom and equality for women
- Lacey

  - first wave grew out of a liberalist concern but used the male standard
  - second wave: 'different but equal'.
- third wave:
  - reflective
  - Understand gender roles and how they operate in the legal and social structures.

14.3 Feminist Views and Universalism

- emphasizes how people deal with circumstances and problems,
- issues of social identity.
- methodology: deconstruction of the perceive 'male' common sense
  - and to create a new way of discussing social and legal issues.
- Universalism present in the suffragette and liberal feminist movements.
- Other movements, cultural feminism, seek a unique and particular subject-formations for women.
- Others attempt to integrate multiple subject-formations .

The Liberal Approach

- Stresses rule of law.
- The second wave of feminism" reveal inequality.
- argues that women should be treated the same.
- Criticism used male-oriented patterns and structures.

The 'Ethics of Care' Approach

- Celebrate gender differences
- Gilligan's two codes.
  - The feminine moral code (The Ethics of Care).
  - The masculine moral code(The Ethics of Justice).
  - In opposition to Kohlberg's work.
- Benhabib :
  - Both moral codes need to be considered together
  - No clear line between private and public life of codes
- Critiques of Gilligan:
  - small sample.
  - global differences?
  - Different socialization?
  - Different biologies?
- West
  - women crave intimacy and connection.
  - liberal legal jurisprudence works against women
  - Need a feminist jurisprudence approach.

Radical Feminist Approaches

- McKinnon
  - Society structured by men to benefit men.
  - This is same as a Marxist power structure.
  - criticizes both the 'sameness' approach and 'difference'
- Criticisms:

  - assumes women are passive victims.
  - attempting to construct universal standard for all women

Ethnic Minority Feminists

- feminist theories neglected social classifications.
- ignored racial and ethnic dimensions of domestic helpers.
- Postmodernists and cultural relativists argue
  - seeking some universal truth of justice for women will fail.
  - thought based in neocolonial and new imperialistic considerations.
- Post-modern feminists
  - reject the idea of 'false consciousness' with fixed identities.
- Other criticize
  - weakens the feminist movements
  - Must set up their own standard of identity to measure inequality

14.4 The Future

- Return to classic progressive political programs
- Some argue that feminism is merely one part of discussing human rights.
- The old liberal theory still valid

About the Author

Dr. Markus McDowell holds a law degree from the University of London. He is the Editor-in-Chief of the *Legal Issues Journal* and writes articles for Legal Yankee, a website of resources for law students in the UK and the US.

www.ingramcontent.com/pod-product-compliance
Lightning Source LLC
LaVergne TN
LVHW022039200926
848481LV00003B/720
* 9 7 9 8 2 1 5 9 1 3 8 1 9 *